A TIME
of WAR

The Inevitable
Conflict Between
the Church of Today
and the Church
of Tomorrow

For foreign and subsidiary rights, contact the author.

Cover design by: Joe De Leon
Cover Photo by: Andrew van Tilborgh

ISBN: 978-1-954089-43-3   1 2 3 4 5 6 7 8 9 10

Printed in the United States of America

A TIME *of* WAR

The Inevitable
Conflict Between
the Church of Today
and the Church
of Tomorrow

MARTIJN VAN TILBORGH

AVAIL

FOREWORD
BY SCOTT WILSON

*"Your system is perfectly designed to get
the results that you are getting."*

I remember the first time I heard that statement. It hit me: *Change isn't going to happen in the church just because we're frustrated at the lack of results. Change will come when we're willing to not only tweak our religious systems, but when we're willing to totally reconstruct them in light of the results we desire to obtain.*

This is exactly what Jesus was talking about in His conversation with John's disciples in Matthew 9:

> *Then John's disciples came and asked him, "How is it that we and the Pharisees fast often, but your disciples do not fast?"*

Jesus answered, "How can the guests of the bridegroom mourn while he is with them? The time will come when the bridegroom will be taken from them; then they will fast.

"No one sews a patch of unshrunk cloth on an old garment, for the patch will pull away from the garment, making the tear worse. Neither do people pour new wine into old wineskins. If they do, the skins will burst; the wine will run out and the wineskins will be ruined. No, they pour new wine into new wineskins, and both are preserved." —Matthew 9:14-17 (NIV)

Three of the Gospel accounts talk about the new wine and new wineskins: Matthew 9, Mark 2, and Luke 5. And they all speak to the same question of John's disciples: why *they* fast and the *Pharisees' disciples* fast but Jesus' disciples don't fast. They want to know, *Why don't you function or govern the same way we do?*

Jesus says, "It's a new day—a new season—because I'm here. The Pharisees' structure is an old wineskin. John the Baptist's structure is an old wineskin. What I'm doing now is something NEW, and it demands a NEW wineskin."

God wants to do a new thing, a new outpouring of His Spirit, but He won't do it until . . . when? Until there is a new wineskin, a new way of thinking, that can hold it. You can pray for an outpouring of God's Spirit, a revival to come. You can sing about the new wine being poured out, but God doesn't pour out new wine into old wineskins. Why? Because the new wine will BREAK the old wineskin, and the new wine will be wasted and lost.

This is exactly what Martijn is talking about in *A Time of War*. He is calling out like a prophet, like Jesus Himself, calling all of us to construct a new wineskin in our thinking that aligns with the outpouring of new wine that God has for us. A great move of God is coming, but it isn't going to come to those who are stuck in their old ways of religious thinking and structure.

I don't know what all of this means. I don't know—and I'm not sure anyone knows—exactly what this new wineskin looks like. But it isn't what we are currently doing right now in the church at large. How do I know? Because we aren't getting the results we want. We are losing ground big-time in America—even in most of the world—and it isn't because the gospel has lost its power. It's because we are still working out of an old wineskin.

Let me ask you: Are you happy with the results you are getting? Are there record numbers of people getting saved in your church? Are you impacting every stream of culture and seeing His kingdom come and His will being done on earth as it is in heaven? If not, would you be willing to do *anything* to see that happen?

Before you answer a big YES too fast, consider the words of Jesus in Luke 5:39 (NIV): "And no one after drinking old wine wants the new, for they say, 'The old is better.'" It's hard for us church leaders to change our thinking and modes of ministry, especially when we feel like we are doing things the way God told us to do them. If we aren't careful, we can fall into the same trap that John's disciples were stuck in—blind to the new thing God IS doing because we are so focused on the old thing God WAS doing.

This book is an amazing wake-up call to all of us who are church/kingdom leaders. After I read it, I cried out to God and asked Him to make my heart pliable, to reshape my thinking in any way He needs to in order for me to receive the new thing He is doing. If you're like I am, you are frustrated with the results we are getting as a church. I want more! But, more and better results can only happen when we're willing to change the way we are doing things. I'm not saying, "Do something new for new's sake." I'm saying, "Let's do the new that God has for us for His kingdom's sake."

Let me pray for you before you start reading, or maybe you'd just want to say this prayer with me:

Father, open our hearts and minds to receive everything You have for us. We don't want to be so busy working for You that we miss the new thing You are doing on the earth and in Your church. Change us into the church You want us to be, so we can see your grace and power move into every sector of society. Whatever we need to do, we are willing to do it. Reveal yourself to us and give us Your wisdom. AMEN.

For more than thirty years, SCOTT WILSON grew Oaks Church into a thriving local ministry in the South Dallas area, with high global impact. Having seen the value of providing a spiritual covering to many church leaders, Scott founded The Father Initiative to raise up spiritual fathers and mothers with a vision that every pastor should have spiritual parents. He also founded Ready Set Grow, a ministry to help churches break through their growth barriers by sharing his own experience and best-in-class partners. Scott has written many books and is a sought-after speaker on personal, spiritual, and organizational growth and leadership. He and his wife, Jenni, have been married since 1990 and have three sons and two daughters-in-law.

CONTENTS

Introduction..13

PART 1. **AT THE CROSSROADS:**
How We Came to This Moment of Decision 17

CHAPTER 1. **THE UNAVOIDABLE CONFLICT:**
Why Change Has to Happen 19

CHAPTER 2. **SEEING THINGS CLEARLY:**
Getting a True Perspective 33

CHAPTER 3. **JUDGES, PRIESTS,
PROPHETS, AND KINGS:**
The Evolution of Godly Leadership 47

PART 2. **A NEW HORIZON:**
Seeing What Needs to Change 65

CHAPTER 4. **A FAITH EARTHQUAKE:**
When Everything Changes 67

CHAPTER 5. **SETTLING FOR SAUL:**
When a Godly Desire is Distorted 85

CHAPTER 6. **NO MORE SECOND BEST:**
Creators, Not Copycats.................... 97

CHAPTER 7. **GOD'S KINGDOM DICTIONARY:**
Learning to Speak His Language 111

CHAPTER 8. **A NEW KIND OF KINGDOM:**
A Family, Not an Institution.............129

PART 3. **A NEW PARADIGM:** Making the Transition 145

CHAPTER 9. **THE KEY TO KINGDOM GROWTH:**
Tearing Down the Walls 147

CHAPTER 10. **A NEW HORIZON:**
Looking at Church Differently 163

CHAPTER 11. **SACRIFICE OVER EXCELLENCE:**
The Heart of Change 175

CHAPTER 12. **TRAINING FOR REIGNING:**
The Hard Path to Kingship 189

THE FUTURE COMES AT A PRICE

Now there was a long war between the house of Saul and the house of David. But David grew stronger and stronger, and the house of Saul grew weaker and weaker. —2 Samuel 3:1

You have probably heard it said that if you keep doing what you have always done, you will get what you have always gotten. That is depressing enough for anyone who believes that God wants more for us. However, it's actually even worse than that because if you just keep doing what you have always done, you will find—after time—that it takes *more* doing of the same to get what you have always gotten.

Doing "the right thing" in the wrong season is counterproductive. Many times, continuing to do the things that provided us with past successes will actually push us into a downward spiral of declining results. It's the law of diminishing returns: You have to pedal harder to maintain your speed.

Therefore, not only will simply doing what we have always done keep us from the bigger future God has in mind, over time, it will prevent us from even maintaining what we have in the present.

For the church to become everything God intends, we're going to have to embrace something called "change." I'm not talking about the kind that doesn't really matter in the big picture— like switching up the color of paint on the walls in your living room or moving the furniture around in your office to create a new look.

Sure, sometimes a freshen-up like that can contribute to a more enjoyable experience and even create a renewed sense of productivity for a time, but it isn't going to make a lasting difference. The kind of change I'm talking about, the kind I believe that is needed to realize what is on God's heart, will be disruptive to every way we've always done things.

It will demand a completely new way of thinking. It will force us to abandon past leadership styles, reject past "best practices," and change our understanding of what it means to be an effective leader.

We will only get to our best future through innovation—not repetition.

TIME TO CHOOSE

Now, I am not saying that we reject everything that has gone before. As church leaders, it's our responsibility to honor the past and look back in history to identify defining moments and enduring principles that got us to where we are today. At the same time, the thing about past victories is that ... well ... they are in the past.

We are called to introduce something new in our generation—something that has never been done. The old tends to precondition our minds to keep us from the new that God wants to do now. The old ways were often good. They produced results. So why leave them behind in pursuit of something else, something uncertain and unproven?

Because the old is our biggest obstacle. Consider what God said through His prophet in Isaiah 43:18-19 (NIV): "Forget the former things; do not dwell on the past. See, I am doing a new thing! Now it springs up; do you not perceive it? I am making a way in the wilderness and streams in the wasteland." He wants us looking up and ahead for what's to come, not down and back at what was.

According to the wisest man who ever lived, there is a time for everything—including conflict. In Ecclesiastes 3:8, Solomon wrote that there is "a time of war, and a time of peace." Some translations phrase it as "a time for war," but that has a significantly different sense. A time *for* war suggests that particular time is for us to initiate, to declare, and there may be occasions when that may be true. But a time *of* war implies that we have no choice in whether or not it will occur. Our decision is what we are going to do when it inevitably breaks out.

I believe that is where we are now in the church. A time of conflict is upon us—an inevitable war between the old and the new. Between the good and the better. Between the church of today and the church of tomorrow.

The only question is this: which side are you on?

I've chosen "tomorrow"! Are you with me?

It won't be easy. The future comes at a price. The odds may even be stacked against us. However, it's a conflict that is worth the risk because victory will push us deeper into the unfolding plan that God has for creation—to see His kingdom manifest on earth as it already is in heaven.

PART ONE

AT THE CROSSROADS:
HOW WE CAME
TO THIS MOMENT
OF DECISION

CHAPTER ONE

THE UNAVOIDABLE CONFLICT: WHY CHANGE HAS TO HAPPEN

We are not the first to find ourselves in "a time of war." Think of when David returned home from leading Saul's army to victory over their enemy. In 1 Samuel 18:6-7 we read:

> Now it had happened as they were coming home, when David was returning from the slaughter of the Philistine[s], that the women had come out of all the cities of Israel, singing and dancing, to meet King Saul, with tambourines, with joy, and with musical instruments. So the women sang as they danced, and said: "Saul has slain his thousands, and David his ten thousands."

It was at that moment that something happened. Something that couldn't be reversed. Angered by the attention being given to David, Saul "eyed David from that day forward" (v. 9).

The women's song became the catalyst of a conflict. A war that would linger on for a long time, but that would eventually be won by David.

If you're really quiet, you can almost hear a similar sound today. It's a song. A song of celebration. A song of victory. A melody that declares the future as it pushes us away from the past, separating us from what once was, but can no longer be. Once you notice this sound, it cannot be unheard. In fact, its volume will amplify as it becomes stronger and stronger in our ears as it seeks to manifest the future in our now.

As leaders, we need to recognize the sound of the song, prophetically discern the times we live in, and embrace the changes that the future demands from us.

The sound is Saul and David in the 21st century. They are prophetic pictures of the church. They represent mindsets, leadership styles, and models that provide revelatory insight into the state of the church. The church of today as well as the church as she could be—as she needs to be—tomorrow.

David represents the future that God has in mind for His people. The prophetic destiny declared over David's life characterizes the very same thing that we are going through in the church today.

David was destined not to perpetuate the kingdom that had been built under Saul, but to accomplish something that had never been done. In fact, the vision that burned inside the heart of David would ultimately erase all that Saul had built over the forty years that he had ruled as king.

I believe that the church finds herself in a similar situation today. We are in a place that we have never questioned before because it is something that has always been there. We grew up in it. It has defined us. It has been part of us, and we've been part of it.

Yet, maybe you have become uncomfortable with it. Unsatisfied with where we—the church—are. You can't quite put a finger on it, but it is there. A sense of unease, that there must be something more. Something better. Something greater that God has in store for His people. Something superior and more enriching.

If this describes you, know that you are not alone. God has awakened a generation destined for greatness beyond what you've ever seen or experienced. A people who will not settle for second best. A people who—despite unlikely circumstances—will choose to believe God and push forward into something that may go down in the history books as one of the deepest church schisms we've ever experienced.

TWO HOUSES, TWO ERAS

Saul's response to David's success raises important questions:

- What was it about David that made Saul so very angry?
- Why was Saul so displeased with the very thing that God had in mind for the future of His people?
- Why did he resist the change that clearly originated from the heart of God Himself?

We will explore the answers to these questions as we dissect the anatomy of the battle between two eras. We will identify areas of conflict between the house of Saul and the house of David, the present and future. We will study what differentiated Saul from David and what exactly caused the incompatibility between the two men as well as the kingdoms they established.

You will discover why Saul and David were never going to be able to coexist long-term. You will understand why this "battle to the death" ended with David as the last man standing.

Now, while David and Saul are archetypes for the church of today, we must remember that we are not fighting against flesh and blood, as Ephesians 6:12 reminds us. I am not suggesting you use the metaphors of Saul and David to point your fingers at the people in your life who may agree or disagree with you and label them accordingly.

Saul and David merely represent the conflict over prophetic alignment with a kingdom paradigm that needs to be uncovered for such a time as this.

There is nothing new under the sun. The battle between the old and the new is as old as Scripture. Ezra 3 tells how the people of Israel were allowed to return from exile to rebuild the temple in Jerusalem. When they gathered to celebrate, there was a mixed reaction:

> But many of the older priests and Levites and family heads, who had seen the former temple, wept aloud when they saw the foundation of this temple being laid, while many others shouted for joy. —Ezra 3:12 (NIV)

Jesus spoke to this sense of division when He was asked why John the Baptist's disciples fasted and His didn't. He answered:

> "And no one pours new wine into old wineskins. Otherwise, the wine will burst the skins, and both the wine and the wineskins will be ruined. No, they pour new wine into new wineskins." —Mark 2:22 (NIV)

In fact, God's Word is full of examples of conflict and tension between the old and the new. As I mentioned in the introduction, the prophet Isaiah pronounced the prerequisite needed in order to see the new thing spring forth: "Do not remember the former things, nor consider the things of old" (Isaiah 43:18).

We, too, must forget the "former things" in order to experience the new thing that God is about to do in our lifetime.

A CLEARER PERSPECTIVE

Before we go more into the prophetic symbolism of the story of Saul and David, we need to take some time to consider why change and disruption of the current state of the church are so important? Why does there need to be conflict? Why can't we just stick to the old ways? Things seem to be going fine the way they are, so why rock the boat?

Let me explain. As leaders, we've been told that we need to remove ourselves from the minutiae of the details and position ourselves at thirty thousand feet, to gain a better vantage point from which to look at the world around us. The thinking is that flying any lower doesn't provide the bird's-eye view we need to see things clearly.

I'd like to propose something different. No, I'm not suggesting that we should lose altitude. As a matter of fact, I want you to consider that maybe you are not flying high enough.

You see, the higher you fly, the farther you can see and the more context you get. Sure, you might lose sight of certain details, but the understanding of the bigger context that you gain may outweigh the loss that you'll experience.

I have come to believe that God is calling us even higher as leaders, to gain visibility on things we couldn't see before, to grasp context crucial to understanding how to position ourselves in our generation.

In Isaiah 46:9-10, God provides us with insight to gain the ultimate bird's-eye perspective we need to lead effectively:

> *"I am God, and there is none like me. I make known the end from the beginning, from ancient times, what is still to come. I say, 'My purpose will stand, and I will do all that I please.'"*

As church leaders, we tend to believe that we—as a generation—are the center of the universe, that both the past and future revolve around us at the epicenter, that the world revolves around us!

This is actually far from the truth. When God declared "the end from the beginning" and "what is still to come," He wasn't just thinking about us.

God doesn't limit Himself to an isolated segment in time, a generation. Rather, He looks at human history as a whole. In His view, our generation is merely a link in a chain of events that pushes creation to *the end*.

There are things that are "still to come" for each generation to do. It's each generation's purpose to manifest new things that will bring us closer to the end. It's our responsibility as leaders to recognize what those things are and to lead our generation to manifest them in context of who we are in history. The word that has been declared from the beginning pushes creation forward consistently, as an invisible force, into new things that are not yet done. God's spoken word pushes creation forward all the time into new things.

We can't escape it. We must yield to it as leaders! What we will leave behind must be different from what we inherit.

The only way to see who we are supposed to be is to fly higher—not to just see what we are to accomplish in our lifetimes, but more importantly, who we are in history and what roles we ought to play in manifesting the things declared from the beginning.

Gaining a higher altitude will inevitably provide us with a perspective that will show us both the need as well as a road map to innovate and reform in our lifetime, rather than to simply maintain (and many times strengthen) the status quo. Our only option is to innovate and ignite a reformation that causes us to advance.

Once you come to peace with the fact that innovation is our only option, you'll start seeing the concept throughout the Bible over and over again.

Let's break this down the word "innovate." According to *Webster's Dictionary*, it means two things:

- a new idea, method;
- the introduction of something new.

Just because we inherited our world from generations past who innovated in their time doesn't mean we're exempt from the responsibility to advance in our generation.

Most leaders agree with this concept. However, true innovation isn't easy. We often pretend to innovate while in reality we are merely adapting to new circumstances or optimizing within an existing paradigm. While adaptation and optimization may create the illusion of progress, we need to understand the difference in order to be effective as leaders.

Before we unpack some more what all that means, let's be clear what innovation is not.

INNOVATION IS NOT ADAPTATION

When circumstances change, we are forced to do something different, not by choice, but because we can no longer do what we used to do because of the new context. We simply reshape what we are familiar with to survive in the new climate. Essentially, it's the same thing we've always done, just a slightly updated version.

We saw a lot of churches adapt during the coronavirus pandemic. They continued to do the same thing they had been doing all along, just an online version of it—the same worship set, the same preaching, the same venue, all just with nobody in the pews.

Now, don't get me wrong. Sometimes we have to adapt to circumstances. Being agile enough to do so when our context changes is important to our survival. However, that's about coping in the "here and now," not creating the future.

I'm not downplaying all the hard work that was involved for churches that "went digital" because of COVID-19, but that kind of adaptation isn't moving the needle of history forward. Nobody is going to look back one hundred years from now and remember how awesome it was when we preached the same sermons over the internet in an empty auditorium.

In the big picture of history, nobody is going to care. It will be remembered as just an inferior version of the same old thing.

INNOVATION IS NOT OPTIMIZATION

Where adaptation shifts us horizontally to a different context, optimization pushes us to a level of excellence within an existing context. It has everything to do with improvement within a current position.

In other words, optimization only happens within a context that already exists. Yes, some change is required to optimize, but not the type of seismic shift that is required to innovate. Change in the context of optimization is vertical. It has everything to do with accomplishing marginal improvement within an existing structure: better communication, better software, better programming, better resources, better facilities and so on.

Optimization doesn't have to be bad, until it becomes bad! It's great to strive for excellence, unless excellence keeps you from moving forward.

There was a reason God instructed Moses to build a tabernacle in the wilderness and not to build a temple. Yes, a temple would have been much nicer than a tent, but it would have kept the people of God from one thing: progress!

When you stay too long in a God-given season, it will ultimately enslave you. Optimization has the ability to do just that. God's people were sent to Egypt by divine instruction so that they could escape a famine. It was a true blessing. However, when they established themselves in that God-given place, they "optimized" their lifestyles while Egypt slowly became their place of confinement, keeping them from moving forward.

INNOVATION DOESN'T JUST HAPPEN

The new doesn't just arrive on one's doorstep, nicely packaged. It has to be pursued, sought out, worked for. It requires courage and true leadership. Progress occurs when we put everything at risk for what has never been done before—something new!

To acquire the type of vision that causes true innovation, we need to fly high—high enough to see the things that are *not yet done*, so that we can make them happen in our generation.

Innovation happens at the edge of chaos. It happens where the developed land stops, and undeveloped land—chaos—starts. It only happens where chaos is cultivated into new opportunities that will advance the kingdom into places it couldn't get before.

Remember, the very definition of innovation is "the introduction of something new." So it will inevitably disrupt the status quo. It can only manifest through reformation of the old, but it doesn't stop there. If we are not careful, we can easily allow this newly cultivated land to become the status quo of tomorrow and potentially keep the next generation from its own inno-vating. We have to keep looking and moving forward.

Let's brave the edge of chaos in our time, and let's manifest something new that the history books will look back on as remarkable.

Innovation is our only option!

CHAPTER TWO

SEEING THINGS CLEARLY: GETTING A TRUE PERSPECTIVE

M any of the 'truths' we cling to depend greatly on our point of view."

These great words were spoken by the legendary *Star Wars* Jedi master, Obi-Wan Kenobi. They are important to reflect on, because, as leaders, we guide others through the lens of what we perceive as truth. Our perception is our reality, and we lead our organizations and ministries accordingly.

The challenge is that, while "perception is reality," as the saying goes, perception is not always a reflection of the truth!

In actuality, it may be more about the context of the moment in a relatively small window of time.

Leadership expert Stephen Covey put it this way: "Each of us tends to think we see things as they are, that we are objective. But this is not the case. We see the world, not as it is, but as we are—or, as we are conditioned to see it."

None of us is exempt from this tendency. We all see the world as we are conditioned to see it by our culture, our history, our upbringing, our experiences, the media, people's opinions, and so on. Our realities can easily get skewed and will therefore deviate from the truth.

As a result, our leadership capacity is limited to the areas where perception and truth overlap. With this in mind, we need to open ourselves to alternative realities beyond our current one so that our perception of the world around us can be aligned with "truth" and we lead more effectively.

Many people would readily agree with this idea, at least in principle. However, in my experience, it is much harder to do than it sounds. Why? Let me attempt to answer that by exploring another story from the Bible.

In Numbers 14:33, we read something that provides profound insight into how perception can keep us from God's promises for our lives and for our generation. God told Moses to tell the people, "And your sons shall be shepherds in the wilderness forty years. . . ."

Here is the context for this verse: After a long journey, God's people had come to the River Jordan. God had delivered them from slavery in Egypt in a powerful way, and through supernatural guidance and intervention, they had miraculously made it to the border of the Promised Land.

Remember that, before they were to cross the Jordan, twelve spies had been sent out to explore the land that God had promised to them. We all know what happened next—ten of the twelve came back with a "bad report," saying that if they crossed the river they were all going to die because the enemies appeared to be much stronger than they were.

The other two spies, Joshua and Caleb, decided to believe God's promise. They encouraged the people to take the land regardless of the overwhelming strength of enemies they would have to conquer.

The people chose to believe the "bad report," and as a result, God decided to keep them in the wilderness for an additional forty years, where those who were twenty years of age or older were destined to die.

Numbers 14:33 refers to the younger generation which ended up being "shepherds in the wilderness for forty years."

Let that sink in. Think about it for a minute. Yes, they would ultimately survive those many years, but to do so they had to become something they were never destined to be: shepherds in the wilderness. By circumstance, not by choice, a whole younger generation was forced to become something they were never supposed to be.

This wasn't just a temporary "season," a short timeout, a brief detour. We're talking about four long decades that ended up defining their very existence.

Everything they did during that time span was the result of something they'd had no control over. The way they acted, the way they thought, and the way their behavior was conditioned were the results of choices another generation had made for them.

Instead of becoming landowners in the land of promise, which was supposed to have happened, they ended up being shepherds in the wilderness. They had no choice. It was the only way to survive their current situation.

Now let me ask you this question: What do you think happens when you are forced, like the Israelites, to become something you were never supposed to be for an extended length of time?

You simply start believing that the life you are living is the one that God has for you, while in reality, there is a whole different world waiting for you beyond the Jordan. You are bound to accept the reality that being a shepherd in the wilderness is in fact the "call" and "destiny" that God has for you.

It's understandable; you simply don't know any better because your whole being has been conditioned to be something you were not supposed to be to the point where you start believing that the life you live is "normal."

If this happened to God's people back then, it can happen to us now.

Could it be that, in a similar way, we, the church, have become "shepherds in the wilderness" today because we have inherited a context that God never intended for us?

Could it be that we now act and lead like shepherds in a place of lack. We talk like shepherds. We think like shepherds. We even train others to be shepherds. Our main goal is now to strive to become the best shepherds possible.

All of this while, in reality, none of us were ever supposed to be shepherds. And by doing so, we're actually strengthening our position in the wilderness.

Apparently, as God's people, it is possible to live and behave long-term under a paradigm of leadership that is in fact contrary to what He has in mind for us.

If this is the case, then we need to "un-shepherd" ourselves and reprogram our thinking to be aligned with the promise across the Jordan. Which brings us back to the conflict between Saul and David.

THE WRONG KIND OF KING

Even though he was anointed by Samuel to become king, Saul was never a king the way God intended—one after His heart, like David would become years later.

Saul's kingship was the result of the Israelites' carnal desire to have a king like the nations around them. 1 Samuel 8:4-5 describes it like this:

> *"Then all the elders of Israel gathered together and came to Samuel at Ramah, and said to him, 'Look, you are old, and your sons do not walk in your ways. Now make us a king to judge us like all the nations.'"*

In other words, God's people demanded a leadership structure that was modeled after the ways of the world. God wasn't interested in that and rejected the idea. Yet the people of Israel insisted that this was the way they wanted to proceed to organize themselves despite all of the negative "side effects" that Samuel warned them about:

> But the thing displeased Samuel when they said, "Give us a king to judge us." So Samuel prayed to the Lord. And the Lord said to Samuel, "Heed the voice of the people in all that they say to you; for they have not rejected you, but they have rejected Me, that I should not reign over them. According to all the works which they have done since the day that I brought them up out of Egypt, even to this day—with which they have forsaken Me and served other gods—so they are doing to you also. Now therefore, heed their voice. However, you shall solemnly forewarn them, and show them the behavior of the king who will reign over them." —1 Samuel 8:6-9

As a result, Saul was anointed as king and, according to Acts 13:21 remained on the throne for . . . forty years. The "shepherds in the wilderness" principle applies here, too: A generation grew up under Saul, yet he was never God's first choice.

Saul was the result of a man-made decision that God ended up tolerating, rather than initiating. He wasn't God's choice; he was the choice of the people—an example of this thing called "freedom of choice" that gets us in trouble from time to time!

Sometimes, wrong choices result in minor consequences. But in this case, the wrong choice resulted in forty years of leadership that was modeled after man-made structures.

Think about the impact of growing up in such a leadership environment. Again, you simply start embracing the culture that has been created. In fact, because you don't know any better, you even tend to perpetuate the very thing that God reject.

If Saul is the only king you have ever known, then what point of reference do you have to desire something better? Saul's kingship is normalized because it's always been like that. For as long as we can remember, everyone around us has "embraced Saul as king" as if he were the ultimate standard of leadership.

SOMETHING AND SOMEONE BETTER

When I look at the church today, I believe we've done quite well under the circumstances. However, I have come to the realization that a lot of what we see today, and a lot of what we've accomplished, has been "under Saul," as it were. A lot of our victories and achievements are the results of initiatives modeled after the ways of the world, just like in Saul's time.

Many churches are looking to the culture around them for ways to do things, rather than seeking God's unique plan. So we have "Christian" versions of what works there, from movies and music to organizations and management.

Like a lot of the kingdom established "under Saul," maybe much of what we have built and created has been borne out of a mindset that was never God's intent. But if Saul has always been your father, you likely don't know any better. If Saul's kingdom is the only one you've ever experienced in your life, then how do you know to look for anything else?

And, one could argue that life under Saul wasn't that bad. After all, he was able to beat enemies nobody else had been able to overcome prior to his rule. He brought a level of strength that no ruler in Israel had ever realized before him. Not Samuel, nor Eli, nor certainly any of the judges had been able to match his leadership capabilities. As Saul defeated thousands of enemies, he had brought the "leadership game" to the next level as the first king of Israel.

Yet something was missing. He was not the man after God's heart that He had in mind for His people. And so a lot of what Saul built was misaligned from what God intended.

As a result, God rejected Saul and chose someone who could really reflect His heart for His people. That is why, in the midst of Saul's reign, the prophets started to speak about "someone better" than he was, as his kingship was rejected by God Himself.

Samuel the prophet told Saul: "The Lord has torn the kingdom of Israel from you today, and has given it to a neighbor of yours, who is better than you" (1 Samuel 15:27).

Soon after, in obscurity, Samuel anointed David as the next king of Israel. While hidden from the public, a new ruler had been appointed by God to be the next king of Israel. A ruler who wasn't only going to be a king for a generation, but someone who would be able to establish a dynasty of kings that would continue from generation to generation.

The song of victory that was heard that day as David came back from battling the Philistines became a declaration of war from Saul against his rival. It was in that moment that Saul realized the prophetic destiny bestowed upon the commander of his army. David had officially become a threat to his kingship.

David was destined not to perpetuate the kingdom that had been built under Saul, but to establish something that had never been done before. In fact, the vision that burned inside the heart of David would ultimately erase all that Saul had built over the forty years that he ruled as king.

This was a point of no return. David knew his destiny. Saul understood what was going on. And to make matters worse, even the people started to recognize and desire a life beyond Saul and to give voice to it through song.

THE JONATHAN DECISION

As I have said previously, David and Saul are not the people in our lives today. They are archetypes. None of us is David or Saul; in fact, we are all Jonathans, sons of Saul. We have all been born under "Saul" and grown up under his leadership.

We were raised in a place that was built by "Saul," a fact that we never questioned before because it was something that had always been there. I know that's true of me: I grew up in it. It defined me. It was part of me. I was part of it. In fact, in part, I helped create it.

But now, like Jonathan, we have a decision to make.

As Saul's natural son, having grown up in the palace, Jonathan was conditioned to think and act like an heir and to follow in his father's footsteps as his successor. To continue the work his father started, in due course.

However, as Jonathan was exposed to David, he soon came to the realization that perpetuating Saul's government wasn't in God's interest, nor in the interest of the people. He even recognized that the future of Israel was with David as king, and he aligned himself with David:

> *Then Jonathan, Saul's son, arose and went to David in the woods and strengthened his hand in God. And he said to*

*him, "Do not fear, for the hand of Saul my father shall
not find you. You shall be king over Israel, and I shall be
next to you. Even my father Saul knows that." So the two
of them made a covenant before the Lord. And David
stayed in the woods, and Jonathan went to his own house.*
—1 Samuel 23:16-18

Like Jonathan, we are caught between two options where each
asks for allegiance. Do we stay loyal to the establishment we
grew up in, or are we going to make a covenant with what God
has declared will be in the future? As time progresses, the pressure
to decide which way you will turn will increase.

Even though the writing was on the wall for Jonathan, and even
though he declared loyalty to David, the tragedy of his life is
that he ultimately died in battle while serving his father Saul.
1 Samuel 31:1-6 tells the story:

*Now the Philistines fought against Israel; and the men
of Israel fled from before the Philistines, and fell slain on
Mount Gilboa. Then the Philistines followed hard after Saul
and his sons. And the Philistines killed Jonathan, Abinadab,
and Malchishua, Saul's sons. The battle became fierce
against Saul. The archers hit him, and he was severely
wounded by the archers. Then Saul said to his armorbearer,
"Draw your sword, and thrust me through with it, lest these
uncircumcised men come and thrust me through and abuse*

me." But his armorbearer would not, for he was greatly afraid. Therefore Saul took a sword and fell on it. And when his armorbearer saw that Saul was dead, he also fell on his sword, and died with him. So Saul, his three sons, his armorbearer, and all his men died together that same day.

The dilemma is real. The religious draw to stay part of the old is strong. Jonathan's sad end demonstrates that even those who have recognized God's prophetic destiny can be pulled back into the past. The old has the ability to put a spell on us. It can be so strong that it pushes us to irrational decisions and loyalty to something that will no longer be.

I'm writing *A Time of War* to help put definition to what you already know on a subconscious level is happening today. To put words to what you're already sensing. And, most importantly to instill the courage that will be needed to break free from the old and pledge allegiance to "the team" that is destined to win.

CHAPTER THREE

JUDGES, PRIESTS, PROPHETS, AND KINGS: THE EVOLUTION OF GODLY LEADERSHIP

Saul and David were very different leaders. One was rejected by God while the other was a man after His heart. What separated them so distinctly? This: King Saul perpetuated the past while King David created a new future. Saul never came into his full kingship. David did.

Let me explain. It's one thing to look back in history and extract "best practices" of past generations and bring them into the present to optimize what you're doing today. It's another thing to look into the future and decide to create something brand new that goes well beyond what the past was able to provide.

Sure, looking back can be valuable as we're trying to learn from past situations. But the past is not where we are going.

As leaders of a new generation, we're called to move into the future while creating something that hasn't been done before. As we study Scripture, it becomes clear that Saul had a hard time letting go of the past. His leadership style, mindset, and methods were largely dependent on past best practices and paradigms.

However, as we've seen in previous chapters, the word that God declared from the beginning pushes us forward into the future to help manifest something new in our generation. As we embrace that assignment, we'll be asked to let go of "the old ways" and allow ourselves to shift into new paradigms of leadership.

When you study the leadership journeys of Saul and David, you discover very quickly that Saul didn't shift at all. He was stuck in old paradigms. In fact, I'd go so far as to say that he was exclusively dependent on the past to function as a leader in his present.

Looking at the generations leading up to Saul and David, we can find residue of the methods, mindsets, and leadership styles of that past. Some of that residue you may recognize even in the church today. Leadership patterns and ideas that seem to be locked in our minds and therefore manifest themselves through behavior that produces sub-par results. Actions that keep us from seeing God's kingdom manifest in ways that He intends.

The problem with Saul was that though he was technically anointed as king, he was conditioned in his mind to operate as a priest and prophet. This was a paradigm embedded in him as a leader because of the past examples he'd learned from. As a result, he never came into his full kingship and was rejected by God.

The leadership model he inherited from the leaders in his past kept him from shifting to the next level, one that would represent God's kingdom on earth. Let's trace that line back:

Before David, there was Saul.

Before Saul, there was Samuel.

Before Samuel, there was Eli.

Before Eli, there were the Judges.

We know that a shift is required for each generation to manifest something new in its time. That shift requires it to detach itself from the past to expand God's kingdom in the future. By studying the leadership history of these different generations, we can clearly identify the crucial shifts that took place in the lives of each of these leaders and the generations they represent.

David prophetically symbolizes the ultimate leader, whom we should learn from and model after. Like you and me, David had his flaws, yet he was able to perpetuate and advance his kingdom throughout both his life as well as the generations following him.

The Bible has a lot of positive things to say about David, but what sums them all up is found in 1 Chronicles 18:6 (NIV):

> *The Lord gave David victory wherever he went.*

Let that sink in for a minute.

David was victorious wherever he went. It didn't matter whom he was fighting; the battle was won. He went through life undefeated!

It may be hard to believe, but this tells me that it's possible to live a life of total victory. One could say that David is the ultimate picture of the victorious church that we should seek to model ourselves after.

So, we must ask ourselves: *Why did David succeed where Saul failed? What was the missing ingredient?*

The answer: Saul was unable to shift.

He was exclusively dependent on past leadership and ministry models—to the point of one time actually calling Samuel back from the dead for advice. This incredible story is found in 1 Samuel 28 and perfectly illustrates why Saul wasn't the king God wanted.

Here's a summary of that story (CEV):

> *Samuel had died some time earlier, and people from all over Israel had attended his funeral in his hometown of Ramah. (v. 1)*

> *His servants told him [Saul], "There's a woman at Endor who can talk to spirits of the dead." (v. 7)*

> *That night, Saul put on different clothing, so nobody would recognize him. Then he and two of his men went to the woman and asked, "Will you bring up the ghost of someone for us?" (v. 8)*

"Who do you want me to bring up?" she asked.

"Bring up the ghost of Samuel," he answered. (v. 11)

Saul knew it was Samuel, so he bowed down low.

"Why are you bothering me by bringing me up like this?" Samuel asked.

"I'm terribly worried," Saul answered. "The Philistines are about to attack me. God has turned his back on me and won't answer any more by prophets or by dreams. What should I do?" (vv. 14-15)

Saul depended on leadership advice from the past to the point of relying on a voice that had literally passed away. Instead of finding what he was looking for, "the past" just reiterated what God had already declared about the future.

Samuel said, "If the Lord has turned away from you and is now your enemy, don't ask me what to do. I've already told you: The Lord has sworn to take the kingdom from you and give it to David. And that's just what he's doing!" (vv. 16-17).

Consider that: Even our past prophetically declares the future!

With that in mind, let's look at each of the generations leading up to Saul and identify its characteristics, some of which you may see certain aspects of in the church today.

JUDGES: TEMPORARY RELIEF FROM TROUBLE

The book of Judges is an interesting collection of stories of leaders who rose up during times of trouble in Israel's history. Many of them are very inspirational and provide us with role models of people who against all odds were able to lead Israel to victory.

However, none of the judges were able to sustain their rule beyond their lifespan. They were uniformly unable to hand the baton to the next generation to continue the positive momentum they were able to create. In some cases, their ministry seems to even have been be cut short mid-life.

They almost appeared as "random moves of God" that sustained His people on their path of survival through history. They weren't particularly anointed with a specific gift like a priest, prophet, or king. They were ordinary people who, for whatever reason, were picked by God to do something remarkable in their lifetimes.

If you're like me and have studied church history, you can see similar moves of God in our past. People like Smith

Wigglesworth, Evan Roberts, Charles Finney, and many others were examples of people who rose up like "judges" in their time to bring temporary "revival" to God's people. Yet nothing remains to this day other than the documented stories originating from those times.

During the days of the judges, God's people were kind of reactively waiting for God to take initiative and select a leader who would offer temporary relief from their oppression.

Residue of that "judges mindset" is still found in the church today as we often tend to wait for God to sovereignly do something in our time.

We call it revival.

Other than praying for it, we don't seem to do much that would cause that revival. All we do is look at the past and point at the "generals" of old who experienced revival in their lifetimes and pray to God to "do it again" in the present. We pray for revival and then wait for it to happen.

It reminds me of the story of the man who was paralyzed for over thirty-eight years at the pool of Bethesda. The story is found in John 5:1-5:

> *After this there was a feast of the Jews, and Jesus went up to Jerusalem. Now there is in Jerusalem by the Sheep*

Gate a pool, which is called in Hebrew, Bethesda, having five porches. In these lay a great multitude of sick people, blind, lame, paralyzed, waiting for the moving of the water. For an angel went down at a certain time into the pool and stirred up the water; then whoever stepped in first, after the stirring of the water, was made well of whatever disease he had. Now a certain man was there who had an infirmity thirty-eight years.

The pool of Bethesda tells the story of the church today. Around the pool of Bethesda *lay a great multitude of sick, blind, lame and paralyzed people* all *waiting* for something to happen. As the church, we often seem to gather together as a group of broken, dysfunctional, sick people who wait for God to do something to make it all better.

Now, of course, we all need Jesus. We all need healing. We all need God to do a miracle in our lives. That's not my point. My point is more that the pathway to receiving that miracle was through WAITING for a miracle. Waiting for a revival.

Life around the pool of Bethesda was based on the stories of those who got healed and the hope that maybe someday it might be one's turn. Other than getting some help from some less sick brothers, all that one could do in Bethesda was simply "wait" and "pray" for a miracle.

Like the man who was paralyzed for over thirty-eight years, our hope today often seems to be limited to the repetition of past experiences as we look at "how God did it before. We also do not realize that the answer to our prayer is standing right beside us.

John 5: 6-8 tells you that story:

> When Jesus saw him lying there, and knew that he already had been in that condition a long time, He said to him, "Do you want to be made well?"
>
> The sick man answered Him, "Sir, I have no man to put me into the pool when the water is stirred up; but while I am coming, another steps down before me."
>
> Jesus said to him, "Rise, take up your bed and walk." And immediately the man was made well, took up his bed, and walked.

Clearly, the man's only hope for healing existed through his believing for history to repeat itself. The only way he could receive healing was through a sovereign move of God, a revival that would happen when the angel would touch the water. *Because that's how God had always done it.*

That's where his focus was. He needed someone to carry him. That was his only hope. And since he didn't have someone to do that for him, he had lost all hope. He couldn't see his miracle.

Like this man, we the church are often fixated on past revivals in hopes that they repeat themselves, while in reality we can't see the answer to our prayer standing right next to us.

If we want to be like David, we have to be like him and shift. We need to start operating at a higher level of thinking. We need to start thinking like a king instead of a judge.

ELI: A RESIDENT PLACE OF MINISTRY

Things changed when Eli became the judge over Israel. When he became the leader over God's people, some intentionality in leadership was restored. Eli wasn't just waiting for God to do something. He knew who he was, and he judged God's people with confidence through that knowledge. He wasn't just some random leader selected by God who would bring temporary relief to the children of God. He was a resident leader who had a sustained and solid ministry for an extended period of time.

Eli was anointed and called for a specific task: to be a priest over Israel. This set him apart from his predecessors. His confidence was instilled by his anointing as priest, and he led accordingly. He knew WHO he was. He knew WHAT he was supposed to do. And he knew WHERE to do it.

As a result he "set up shop" in Shiloh, where he ministered in the tabernacle until the day he died. During that time, he saw a measure of success his predecessors never did. He was able to create an environment that served God's people consistently for about forty years. A resident presence of God existed in his place of ministry for most of them. The ark of the covenant was permanently present in Eli's place of government.

There was a system to his success. You may recognize much of this pattern in the church today.

However, Eli's leadership ability was limited to his anointing as a priest. He was not a king like David, nor a prophet like Samuel. As a result, he was not able to rule God's people through a kingdom paradigm. Within the limited capacity of his anointing as priest, he was able to minister to God's people from Shiloh where the tabernacle and the ark were located. If you ever needed a breakthrough, Eli was ready for you to come to his meeting to pray for a miracle.

This is exactly what happened to Hannah, who was barren. She prayed to God, and her breakthrough came because she was able to "go to church" (Shiloh) and have the "man of God" (Eli) pray for her miracle.

The "Eli ministry and leadership model" is limited to people attending our meetings in order to experience a breakthrough. A genuine, God-initiated breakthrough, to be sure, but one that's limited due to the fact that it only happens in a certain place.

Much of our ministry today is modeled after Eli. As the church, we establish a presence in a specific location we call "a local church" and invite people who need a breakthrough to "come get their miracle" in our meetings. And even though miracles happen there, the big picture impact advancement of God's kingdom is minimal.

The priestly anointing is simply not enough to fulfill our mandate as the church and to see God's kingdom established on earth. We need another shift. One that takes us beyond the priestly model of ministry into a kingdom mindset. A shift that increases our influence. A shift that helps us win battles that we previously were unable to win.

SAMUEL: EXPANDING INFLUENCE

The first thing that Samuel did after Eli had died was relocate. After he recaptured the ark of the covenant, he packed his bags and moved to a new city called Ramah, which he made his residence.

When you look on the map, it's interesting to see that this geographical move put him closer to Jerusalem, which ultimately became the seat of government for King David. Samuel wasn't a king though. He was a prophet who grew up amid a priestly order of government.

However, Samuel knew that his destiny was to not simply perpetuate Eli's ministry. That's why he shifted and expanded his influence beyond just Shiloh. You might say that Samuel operated the first ever multi-campus ministry. 1 Samuel 7:15-17 tells the story:

> *And Samuel judged Israel all the days of his life. He went from year to year on a circuit to Bethel, Gilgal, and Mizpah, and judged Israel in all those places. But he always returned to Ramah, for his home was there. There he judged Israel, and there he built an altar to the Lord.*

As you can see, from his main campus in Ramah, Samuel expanded his ministry into three other territories. He wasn't just waiting for people to show up in Ramah. God had called and sent him to other places as well. Within his anointing as a prophet he was somehow able to manifest God's presence in specific places that he felt God had called him to. Samuel wasn't limited to one place. He went to specific places that God had put on his heart and judged Israel from there.

Unfortunately, the prophetic anointing is simply not enough to fulfill our mandate as the church. Another shift is still needed. One that takes us beyond both the Eli and the Samuel models of ministry. A shift that increases our influence to win battles we couldn't win before. A shift that allows us to rule as kings and that will see His kingdom be established on earth as it already is in heaven.

SAUL: STUCK IN THE PAST

Sadly, Saul never became that king. Even though he was anointed as king, the way he operated as a leader was limited to what he had learned from Samuel, Eli, and the judges before him. His behavior as a leader never aligned with his true anointing as a king.

He didn't shift.

Saul was stuck in old behaviors and past leadership paradigms which resulted in a rapidly growing toxic spiritual climate for God's people. It was an environment that ultimately became a catalyst of the war between the house of Saul and the house of David.

There is no record of Saul making a shift of any kind. He just reactively became king, which in reality didn't do much good for God's people.

It is interesting to note Saul's relationship with the ark of the covenant. Where the ark was a priority for both Eli and Samuel, Saul essentially ignored God's presence throughout his whole reign as king.

1 Samuel 7:1-2 tells how Samuel had recaptured the ark from the Philistines and put it into the care of Eleazar:

*Then the men of Kirjath Jearim came and took the ark of
the Lord, and brought it into the house of Abinadab on the
hill, and consecrated Eleazar his son to keep the ark of the
Lord. So it was that the ark remained in Kirjath Jearim a
long time; it was there twenty years.*

For two decades the ark remained untouched. It stayed exactly
where Samuel had placed it until David picked it up after he
was anointed king by the people of Israel, as told in 2 Samuel
6. What does this tell us? That the presence of God was not
central, not crucial to Saul's kingship.

He ended up ruling as a king but without truly walking in his
anointing as a king. His ministry had a sense of true kingship
while in reality, over time it became a false representation of
what God's kingdom was supposed to look like. He compen-
sated by borrowing old methods that belonged to other leaders
from the past to make up for his lack in leadership.

To sum it up, Saul never shifted. He was not a true king, he was
a KINO: King in Name Only!

When you carry the title of a king but do not truly shift into
your anointing as a king, you'll end up misrepresenting the
kingdom you're supposed to be leading.

Saul ended up being a king in name only, but he was the only
king the people had ever known. So God's people treated him as

a true king. Little did they know that the true king had joined Saul's worship team and was playing the harp in Saul's palace!

It wasn't until David came home from battle one day that the people started to notice the difference between him and Saul. It was in that moment that a song separated the house of Saul from the house of David forever, as a true king had manifest himself through battle.

A conflict had been born that would grow to a full-out war. The same war that we are in the middle of today, the war between the church of today and the church of tomorrow.

PART TWO

A NEW HORIZON:
SEEING WHAT NEEDS TO CHANGE

CHAPTER FOUR

A FAITH EARTHQUAKE: WHEN EVERYTHING CHANGES

The biggest mistake that we can make is to try to build a kingdom in Shiloh or Ramah. Eli and Samuel were good men, but they were unable to administrate a kingdom simply because they were not kings. They facilitated a place and model of government, just not the type of government adequate enough to administrate a kingdom.

Such was also the case with Saul, a king in name only. He was the result of the people's demand for a king—a desire that was planted by God, yet misinterpreted by the people. Saul was anointed to be king, but he never took his true position.

He never shifted. Instead he remained dependent on previous forms of government.

Essentially, one could say that Saul tried to be a king in Ramah. But Ramah was the seat of government for Samuel the prophet; it didn't facilitate the right environment for a king. It was too limited. Saul failed to see that and tried to administrate a kingdom from a Ramah position and perspective. To administrate a kingdom, Saul had to move away from the establishment of the day. By failing to do so, he set himself up to fail as a king.

A kingdom culture can't exist within our current church culture, just as Saul could not fully rule as a king in Ramah. This is something extremely important to understand. We can't bring kingdom culture to the church. We need to bring our churches to kingdom culture. There's a crucial difference.

Remember, Saul, the first king of Israel, tried to fit into what already existed instead of bringing everything that already existed into a new paradigm.

I call this the discrepancy between prophetic revelation and apostolic manifestation. Just because you perceive certain things on a revelatory or prophetic level, doesn't mean you are actually operating according to that revelation. In other words, just because we understand the importance and relevance of God's kingdom, doesn't mean we are actually aligned with the revelation of it.

Saul understood that God wanted a kingdom. He was anointed as a king. People called him a king. And, most importantly, God had prophetically spoken over his life that he was chosen to be the king of Israel.

Yet despite the overwhelming evidence of what should be, Saul conformed to what already was. He never shifted. On a practical level not much changed. In fact, one could argue that things got worse—way worse—under Saul.

Just because we perceive something doesn't mean we have transitioned and aligned ourselves with what we see. It is given for a reason. Revelation demands action that will move us away from our current reality into a new better normal. As the church, we have to find the courage to move away from established ways of doing things and align ourselves with what we know God wants to do in our generation. We need to be willing to leave Shiloh and Ramah behind and move to Jerusalem, a place unknown to us. A city that operated by a different set of rules.

I've become convinced that a lot of "failure" that we've seen in the church is the result of this very principle. The right person with the right anointing with the right calling in the wrong context will operate under tremendous pressure that can manifest in a wide variety of bad ways.

Personally, I believe the flaws that Saul displayed throughout his life were the result of the pressure of being set up to fail. Now, that doesn't justify his behavior. Of course Saul was responsible for his choices and decisions. I'm just saying that the environment that was the result of not shifting made him snap at times.

When you cage a king, you'll see the worst of him manifest under that pressure.

Putting a generation of kings in a place that is not conducive to a kingdom will do exactly the same.

Consider the following account in 2 Kings 6:1-6 (emphasis added):

> *And the sons of the prophets said to Elisha, "See now, the place where we dwell with you is too small for us. Please, let us go to the Jordan, and let every man take a beam from there, and let us make there a place where we may dwell."*
>
> *So he answered, "Go."*
>
> *Then one said, "Please consent to go with your servants."*
>
> *And he answered, "I will go."*

So he went with them. And when they came to the Jordan,
they cut down trees. But as one was cutting down a tree, the
iron ax head fell into the water; and he cried out and said,
"Alas, master! For it was borrowed."

So the man of God said, "Where did it fall?" And he showed
him the place. So he cut off a stick, and threw it in there; and
he made the iron float. Therefore he said, "Pick it up for
yourself." So he reached out his hand and took it.

For me, this passage clearly illustrates what we're going
through in our generation.

Here were what verse one calls the "sons of the prophets" who
came to Elisha the prophet. What we see is a new generation of
leaders raised by Elisha the prophet who had come to a conclusion: That *the place where we dwell with you is too small for us.* Isn't
that exactly what we're talking about?

FINDING A LARGER PLACE

Saul the king, who was raised by Samuel the prophet, found
himself in a place which was "too small" to be a king in.

As a generation of kings, we have to come to the same conclusion. The place in which we were raised has become too small
for us. It's not conducive to help us become truly who we are
supposed to be as kings.

So here were the sons of the prophets explaining to Elisha that they felt constricted by the status quo. The new generation was asking permission to leave their "hometown" and go to a new place that they envisioned for themselves.

I'm not sure what I would have done in Elisha's situation. There he was, having spent his life raising a generation of leaders. He trained them. He equipped them. He taught them everything they knew. And now they were complaining about how constricted they felt. They just wanted to leave the place where they had always been with Elisha. They just wanted to get out. It wasn't satisfactory to them.

Surprisingly, Elisha didn't get offended. He didn't get angry. He didn't misunderstand. In fact, he discerned what was really going on and gave them permission to go!

He realized that if the next generation was truly going to be and do all that God had for them he just had to let them move away from what they had known for all those years. He knew that what had always been could not be part of the future. He had to let it go.

As a result he simply responded with a two-letter word: "Go" (v. 2).

And as Elisha gave permission to the next generation to go, something remarkable happened. The sons of the prophet turned around and invited him to be part of the new: "Please consent to go with your servants" (v. 3).

The sons didn't try to fit into the existing world, but they invited the existing world with them into the new dwelling place that they were creating.

As a Davidic generation, we're called to be kings. We're called to administrate a kingdom. This cannot happen within the existing context of "church." Like the sons of the prophets, the place where we currently dwell has become too small for what we should be.

Instead of trying to "fit in," we should invite the past to become part of the new future that we're creating. Not to perpetuate the past in the future, but to recontextualize some of what the past has offered us as part of the new normal.

Elisha agreed and also decided to leave the dwelling that he had been in for all of his life. He decided to move into the future by following a new generation of leaders. Yes, things were going to be different, but by Elisha recognizing the season of God, it allowed him to be a blessing to that new generation.

In due course, Elisha was able to share wisdom and counsel that would allow him to help the young leaders to solve a challenge they were encountering as they were building their new dwelling. He provided valuable insight that helped them recover the ax head that had gotten lost along the way.

We have to learn from this.

Yes, we have no option but to pack our bags and leave our current dwellings. But in going, we should invite those who raised us to be part of the new future we're creating.

The place where we dwell has become too small.

A NEW HORIZON

I remember the time that God confronted me with a question that rocked my world. It was during a season when I was involved in church planting. In fact, I was part of church plants in five different cities (I don't recommend it!) in the Netherlands, where I grew up. Somehow, I managed to have a full-time job during the day, driving around the country in the evenings and on the weekends to develop these different congregations.

During this period, I grew rapidly more frustrated with my situation, needing a full-time job to pay the bills. I didn't really complain about it, but deep down inside I felt a growing resentment toward God about the situation. Here I was, doing His work, while needing this job that I definitely didn't enjoy to support my family.

If I was working for Him, why couldn't He take better care of me?

Then, out of the blue one day, I felt the Holy Spirit asking me the following question: *What are you doing?*

At first I didn't understand, so I asked Him to elaborate. The same question came back to me a second time: *What are you doing?*

My response? *You know what I am doing! I'm planting churches. Five churches, to be exact. Remember?*

This answer started a conversation with God that altered the trajectory of my life completely. He started to challenge me on my answer:

Say what? I don't understand?

So, I found myself explaining again to God what it was I was doing for Him: *I'm planting churches. Remember?*

He proceeded to question me about these activities I claimed to be involved in on His behalf: *Can you explain? I'm not sure if I understand!*

This was getting really ridiculous really fast.... Why was God asking me such annoying questions? He knew exactly what it was I was doing.

I should have realized right then and there that when God asks you a question it's probably not because He doesn't know the answer. He was asking the question to tell me something.

So, for the third time, I attempted to communicate to God how I was working so hard for Him to plant all these churches. Then I proceeded to elaborate by explaining to Him what church planting was: *You know . . . you go to a city, or a town, you find a place. Then you call a meeting and invite people. You sing and preach. . . .*Midway through my explanation, I felt the Lord saying something that totally rocked my world.

Hmmm . . . interesting concept . . . I had never heard of church planting before. Thanks for explaining.

It was in that moment that I realized two things: First, my life was consumed with activity and effort that He had never asked me to be involved in. He had never mandated I plant any church. Ever.

Second, the "activity" of "church planting" wasn't even something in the Bible. There is no reference whatsoever to "church planting" found in the Word of God.

Crazy, right?

Yet, for some reason, I had never questioned the activities that had consumed my time, energy, and money for such an extended period of time.

GOD'S KINGDOM MANDATE

I started to realize that God Himself actually assumes responsibility for building His church. He never wanted us to be responsible for that to begin with.

In Matthew 16:18, Jesus says: "*I will build My church,*" (emphasis added).

Never had I considered whether or not I should be planting and building churches on His behalf. This realization didn't just disrupt the journey I was on, but the trajectory of what I had envisioned the rest of my life to look like.

I continued to pray through my conversation with God and quickly came to the conclusion that what He was asking from me was very simple—something that had been "hiding in plain sight" all along. I had just never seen it this way.

What God had asked from me was not to help Him plant a bunch of churches but to help Him establish His kingdom on earth!

Let me repeat that in different words. Sure, God wants a church, but He doesn't want us to be responsible for building it. However, as the church, He does want us to share the responsibility of governing His kingdom on earth.

I had never seen it this way. But as I read Scripture, I suddenly saw it everywhere.

All that God has ever wanted was a kingdom on earth. And everything that He has ever done since the beginning of creation has been to establish His kingdom on earth as it already is in heaven.

It started in the Garden of Eden, where He placed man and gave him the authority to rule on His behalf and expand His domain across the face of the earth (Genesis 1:26).

The story of David is a story of that same kingdom that God had in mind from the beginning of time. The history of David and his journey to kingship prophetically foreshadows the same journey we are on as His people today.

As His people, we are destined to be kings in His kingdom.

Suddenly, I saw that "the kingdom" was all that Jesus ever talked about. Literally EVERYTHING He ever shared tied back to that kingdom. His parables, His preaching, His conversation with Nicodemus, His prayers . . . literally EVERYTHING He ever said and did related one way or the other to the kingdom that God wants us to be part of.

Here are just a few of the countless examples from Scripture that I found:

- "But seek *the kingdom* of God, and all these things shall be added to you." (Luke 12:31, emphasis added)
- "Do not fear, little flock, for it is your Father's good pleasure to give you *the kingdom*." (Luke 12:32, emphasis added)
- "Repent, for *the kingdom* of heaven is at hand." (Matthew 4:17, emphasis added)
- "And Jesus went about all Galilee, teaching in their synagogues, preaching the gospel of *the kingdom*, and healing all kinds of sickness and all kinds of disease among the people." (Matthew 4:23, emphasis added)
- "Your *kingdom* come. Your will be done On earth as it is in heaven." (Matthew 6:10, emphasis added)
- "Then Jesus went about all the cities and villages, teaching in their synagogues, preaching the gospel of *the kingdom*, and healing every sickness and every disease among the people." (Matthew 9:35, emphasis added)
- "Another parable He put forth to them, saying: 'The *kingdom* of heaven is like a man who sowed good seed in his field.'" (Matthew 13:24, emphasis added)

- "Unless one is born again, he cannot see *the kingdom* of God." (John 3:3, emphasis added)

- "Now it came to pass, afterward, that He went through every city and village, preaching and bringing the glad tidings of *the kingdom* of God." (Luke 8:1, emphasis added)

- "He sent them to preach *the kingdom* of God and to heal the sick." (Luke 9:2, emphasis added)

- "But when the multitudes knew it, they followed Him; and He received them and spoke to them about *the kingdom* of God, and healed those who had need of healing." (Luke 9:11, emphasis added)

- "Jesus said to him, 'Let the dead bury their own dead, but you go and preach *the kingdom* of God.'" (Luke 9:60, emphasis added)

- "For *the kingdom* of God is not in word but in power." (1 Corinthians 4:20, emphasis added)

- "For so an entrance will be supplied to you abundantly into the everlasting *kingdom* of our Lord and Savior Jesus Christ." (2 Peter 1:11, emphasis added)

- "Now salvation, and strength, and *the kingdom* of our God, and the power of His Christ have come, for the accuser of our brethren, who accused them before our God day and night, has been cast down." (Revelation 12:10, emphasis added)

Again, this is just a quick sampling of an incredible number of biblical references to the kingdom of God. This kingdom is what it's all about. As Jesus builds His church, He wants us to understand how to administrate His kingdom on earth.

A CLASH OF CULTURES

Why is this kingdom emphasis so important to understand? Isn't it just a difference in terminology?

Church?

Kingdom?

What's the difference? Does it really matter? Aren't we all talking about the same thing?

Well, let me put it this way. When God started to show me that His whole agenda was centered around establishing His kingdom on earth, it created a conflict on the inside of me— one that challenged everything I knew was right.

It challenged how I spent my time. How I spent my money. And how I spent my energy. Honestly, it challenged what I believed was my very life's purpose.

That conflict I experienced was, in essence, the same one that occurred between Saul and David, and it is the same one we find ourselves in today.

It is a conflict between what I call "church culture" and "kingdom culture."

Yes, I know the words "kingdom culture" are way overused. Many of us have become numb to them. But their meaning has over time morphed into something that it's not. The bottom line is that as the church, we find ourselves in a culture shift. A shift between church culture into kingdom culture.

Previously, we talked about "shifts" and how Saul never shifted after he was anointed king. Saul exclusively depended on the past in his attempt to rule.

David knew one thing: As a true king anointed by God to rule His kingdom, he had to shift. Shift away from the things of old into a new place of authority and leadership that previous generations were unable to attain. He had to ascend to a higher level of government. A new location. A better place.

It was a shift that would open up possibilities to see victories beyond Shiloh and Ramah and would allow the house of David to expand his influence beyond limitations that previous generations had been conditioned by. A shift that now demands we move from a church to a kingdom mindset. A shift that requires us to create a true kingdom culture.

The war between the house of Saul and the house of David was a war about the same shift we're going through as the church today.

It is one that will end up shifting God's people to a new form of government. It will catapult us into a different era that will allow us to not only compete with other nations, but ultimately experience victories wherever we go, just as David did.

CHAPTER FIVE

SETTLING FOR SAUL: WHEN A GODLY DESIRE IS DISTORTED

Before we take a closer look at what it will mean for us to establish a new, kingdom culture, we need to address one common objection to what I have said so far. Many resist the idea of a kingdom culture like David's because, they say, God never intended for Israel to have a king in the first place.

I can see how some may come to this conclusion from a reading of 1 Samuel 8, telling the history of God's people demanding a king. On the surface, it really looks like they had lost their minds and that God in a moment of frustration just "gave them what they wanted." And while there is an element of truth to this, I have discovered that there is a deeper understanding to be gained of the situation.

Sometimes things are not quite what they seem. And when we carefully study the story of Saul and David, there are a few nuances we have to pay attention to.

Let's revisit this story and take a closer look at what really happened when God's people demanded a king. The account is to be found in 1 Samuel 8:4-21:

> Then all the elders of Israel gathered together and came to Samuel at Ramah, and said to him, "Look, you are old, and your sons do not walk in your ways. Now make us a king to judge us like all the nations." But the thing displeased Samuel when they said, "Give us a king to judge us." So Samuel prayed to the Lord.

> And the Lord said to Samuel, "Heed the voice of the people in all that they say to you; for they have not rejected you, but they have rejected Me, that I should not reign over them. According to all the works which they have done since the day that I brought them up out of Egypt, even to this day—with which they have forsaken Me and served other gods—so they are doing to you also. Now therefore, heed their voice. However, you shall solemnly forewarn

them, and show them the behavior of the king who will reign over them."

So Samuel told all the words of the Lord to the people who asked him for a king.

And he said, "This will be the behavior of the king who will reign over you: He will take your sons and appoint them for his own chariots and to be his horsemen, and some will run before his chariots. He will appoint captains over his thousands and captains over his fifties, will set some to plow his ground and reap his harvest, and some to make his weapons of war and equipment for his chariots. He will take your daughters to be perfumers, cooks, and bakers. And he will take the best of your fields, your vineyards, and your olive groves, and give them to his servants. He will take a tenth of your grain and your vintage, and give it to his officers and servants. And he will take your male servants, your female servants, your finest young men, and your donkeys, and put them to his work. He will take a tenth of your sheep. And you will be his servants. And you will cry out in that day because of your king whom you have chosen for yourselves, and the Lord will not hear you in that day."

Nevertheless the people refused to obey the voice of Samuel; and they said, "No, but we will have a king over us, that we also may be like all the nations, and that our king may judge *us and go out before us and fight our battles." And Samuel heard all the words of the people, and he repeated them in the hearing of the Lord.*

So the Lord said to Samuel, "Heed their voice, and make them a king."

It's an intriguing story, isn't it? On the surface it appears that "the people" were completely off their rockers. That they reached the state of ultimate rebellion.

Yet, it's complicated!

WEARY HEARTS, WRONG CONCLUSIONS

Even though they asked for the wrong thing, I believe that there was a lot "right" in what they asked at the same time. There was more going on under the surface that caused them to make the request to Samuel.

In verse 4 we read the people told Samuel, "Now make us a king to judge us like all the nations." The key words here are *like all the nations*. It wasn't so much that they demanded a king, per se, as that they demanded a king like all the nations around them.

The people were looking at other dynasties around Canaan and they felt like they couldn't compete.

The other nations that surrounded them had more power, more influence, more wealth, better military, better weapons.

Better EVERYTHING, really.

The people of Israel wanted what the other nations had . . . and more. How come they were God's people yet they had less than what the other nations had? It simply didn't make sense to them.

They read the scriptures and they taught their kids what Moses had told them. Things like:

> *"You shall lend to many nations, but you shall not borrow. And the Lord will make you the head and not the tail; you shall be above only, and not be beneath."*
> —*Deuteronomy 28:12-13*

For many years they had memorized these promises, meditated on them, and held on to them as they were trying to envision the future that God had for them. Yet, there seemed to be an overwhelming discrepancy between what God had said about their destiny and their current reality.

How come "other nations" who didn't have a covenant with God Almighty were experiencing more of what they believed God had for His people than they did?

The Bible says that "hope deferred makes the heart sick" (Proverbs 13:12). God's people had hoped for a better future for too long. Their hope had been deferred to the point where their hearts had grown weary.

Looking for answers. they started to believe that the other nations knew something they didn't. These other peoples must be doing something right that they were doing wrong.

The only thing that they could conclude while analyzing the other nations was that they had something the Israelites did not.

Kings!

Never in its history had Israel had a king. A king must be the missing link between the Israelites' current reality and their future destiny. They needed a different form of government. A monarchy would be the answer.

So, to get what Scripture said they should have, they needed a king like the other nations had kings.

Besides, only a king can compete with other kings.

You can only compete if you're playing the same game. Up until now, they had been playing a different game altogether.

They had come to the conclusion that a priest (Eli) or a prophet (Samuel) would never be able to compete with a king; therefore, they needed one just like those other nations had.

Now, here is the tricky part. Just because God rejected the idea of having a king *like the other nations*, it didn't mean that He rejected the idea of a monarchy altogether.

In fact, as we already discovered, God has wanted a kingdom all along!

The kingdom that God has had in mind, however, doesn't have the same characteristics that the kings of other nations were displaying.

He wanted a King—just not one like the other nations.

A GODLY DESIRE TO RULE

The big-picture reality is that the main storyline of Scripture is all about God's kingdom. As we have noted previously, God gave man authority over His domain in the Garden of Eden when He told Adam and Eve to subdue it and have dominion.

The King of Kings gave His people authority over His domain. In fact, the very word "kingdom" speaks about the "*king's domain*."

He made us rulers of His domain, making us effectively kings within His kingdom.

The Bible talks about Jesus being the "King of kings" on multiple occasions. So who are those kings He is King over?

He talks about *us* being those kings!

George MacDonald was a Scottish minister and writer of fiction and prose of the 1800s who preceded and influenced C. S. Lewis, among others. In *Unspoken Sermons*, he wrote (emphases added):

> *What then is the kingdom over which the Lord cares to reign, for he says he came into the world to be a king? I answer, a kingdom of kings, and no other.* Where every man is a king, *there and there only does the Lord care to reign, in the name of his Father. The Lord cares for no kingdom over anything this world calls a nation. A king must rule over his own kind. Jesus is a king in virtue of no conquest, inheritance, or election, but in right of his essential being.* His subjects must be of his own kind, in their very nature and essence kings.

Remember, God created us in His image. If He is a King and we are created in His image, then He effectively created us to operate like kings in His kingdom.

Because of the genesis of God's kingdom and what His intended purpose was with creation, I believe He deposited a desire, a drive, in every human being to rule and reign.

The Word of God declared in the Garden of Eden planted the desire for kingship in every person. That desire drives mankind to create, subdue, and expand influence. We are all destined to be kings in His kingdom.

Outside of a relationship with God, that desire can be a bad thing. Yet when aligned with God's eternal purpose to expand His kingdom, it can be a very powerful and positive thing.

In fact, without it, we are unable to fulfill our God-given purpose as His people. Without it we're unable to live up to the promises of Scripture. Without it we are unable to even compete with those who live without God.

The problem is that you can't put a generation of people who are called to be kings in a place like Shiloh or Ramah. They are the product of a different form of government. One that possibly was needed during a certain time and era to move God's people forward from where they were, but one where they should not stay indefinitely.

Shiloh and Ramah were places where the status quo of leadership was executed by a priest or prophet. When you're destined to be a king, you can't function in such a place. Sooner or later it will create problems.

A king in Shiloh will either break Shiloh or be broken himself.

Kings need to be among kings. They want to compete on their level. If you're born to be a king, you don't want to be put in an environment that can't allow you to be a king.

I have come to believe that the root of the dissatisfaction of the people during Samuel's reign was a good one; they desired something more than what they were currently experiencing under Eli and Samuel. Something deep inside told them that there had to be more than their current reality.

They were frustrated with the fact that the nations around them were doing better than they were. Other nations saw more success and experienced bigger and better things then they did. How come they, who had a covenant with God, experienced a lower quality of life then those around them who didn't have that same relationship with Him?

The Israelites' desire for more than what they were experiencing was a genuine and good one. It was a desire that God had placed inside them. A desire to rule as kings.

Their interpretation of what they believed they needed in order to see that desire come to pass, however, was a misinterpretation of the situation.

But how could they know? They had never had a king. The only kings they had ever seen were those of other nations.

So, yes, they were wrong in their demands. But who could really blame them? They simply didn't know better. There was no point of reference to what a godly king should be like. All they knew about monarchy was what other nations around them were showing them.

There is other evidence in Scripture that God wanted His people to have a king (just not one like the other nations). During the days of Eli, a prophet showed up and prophesied about David, the man after God's own heart:

> *"Now this shall be a sign to you that will come upon your two sons, on Hophni and Phinehas: in one day they shall die, both of them. Then I will raise up for Myself a faithful priest who shall do according to what is in My heart and in My mind. I will build him a* sure house, *and he shall walk before My anointed forever."* —1 Samuel 2:34-35 *(emphasis added)*

As God judges Eli's house, He also previews what's going to come down the road. He gives us some insight into the future leadership of Israel. And even though God calls this faithful leader a priest, he also tells him He will build him a "sure house."

These two words in the original text imply that God will build a "royal dynasty" through this person. The prophet is talking about David who becomes the first true king—a king who produced a dynasty that didn't only bring the Messiah, but also ultimately us, the kings in His kingdom.

Yes, God's kingdom will have priests and prophets, but the dominant model of government is a kingdom.

We are called to be kings, but we are part of an environment that operates like Shiloh and Ramah. We will never be able to reach our full potential if we stay there. The church of today will have to shift into the church of tomorrow.

Deep down inside, we know there is more. We know things have to change. We know we can't stay where we've been.

We must ask ourselves this: *Are we willing to do what it takes to get there?*

CHAPTER SIX

NO MORE SECOND BEST: CREATORS, NOT COPYCATS

To be perfectly honest with you, I am disappointed.

Disappointed with the inability that we, the church, have to really make an impact on the world around us.

It seems that we always come in second. Never do we seem to be part of the winning team.

I know, I know. I am not supposed to say these things because the Bible tells us we are "more than conquerors" (Romans 8:37).

But I have to be honest with myself. I can no longer deny what I know. We, the church, have NOT been victorious. We have NOT been on the winning team. We have NOT made the impact we were supposed to make. We are NOT that city on a hill that shines its light into the darkness.

We simply are not!

When it comes to creating culture and advancing society, we have tried hard and seen some progress, but we seem to always miss the podium when it comes to medal time.

Now, I don't want to be a Debbie Downer, but at the same time I don't want to pretend either. I feel like the little boy in the story of the emperor who has no clothes: I can't deny what I see.

For too long we've convinced ourselves that the life we experience today is the one that God has for us, while in reality there is so much more!

It's our responsibility to get to "the more" and to demonstrate "the more." If we don't, we simply misrepresent God to the world around us.

Matthew 13:44 says: "Again, the kingdom of heaven is like treasure hidden in a field, which a man found and hid; and for joy over it he goes and sells all that he has and buys that field."

We tell people that we have found this treasure hidden in a field while in reality it's a box of rocks. And then we try to convince ourselves that it's worth selling all we have to acquire it.

But when I look around and see what we have accomplished as the church, I have to draw the conclusion that it's simply not worth it.

If this is IT, I have better things to do, to be brutally honest! Don't you?

Don't misunderstand: I'm happy that Jesus loved me enough to do what He did. But I can't escape the feeling that what He died for is so much more than what we're experiencing today. If "going to heaven" is all we're getting out of His sacrifice, then we are undervaluing what He did.

Luke 12:32 says that it is "your Father's good pleasure to give you the kingdom." Once saved, we have access to that kingdom. Not doing so is disrespectful to the One who paid the price to get it for us. And even if we don't want it for ourselves, the world around us needs it.

In the previous chapter, I referenced Deuteronomy 28:13, which says that "the Lord will make you the head and not the tail." But the reality is that we're the tail—not the head. The world around us is the head and we, the church, are simply following suit. We are following the other kings.

We have determined that "Eli" and "Samuel" don't provide us with the proper infrastructure and environment to really become the head. A priest and a prophet can do a lot, but they can't set us up to become kings in an environment that thrives, grows, and advances continuously.

We have to move away from Shiloh and Ramah to become all God has created us to be ... kings in His kingdom!

The key is to develop a kingdom culture that will facilitate an environment that allows us to be like David and win battles everywhere we go (1 Chronicles 18:6). Until then, we will lag behind the world in every aspect of culture.

Some say that culture is created through the seven spheres of influence that are present in every society:

- Arts and entertainment
- Business and the economy
- Education
- Family
- Government
- Media
- Religion

There may be more, but these different spheres are sectors of influence that we, the church, need to position ourselves in in order to truly become impactful on society.

Think for a moment about how we are doing in each of these spheres.Exactly! Instead of setting the tone, we're merely following suit. Copying what we see. As a result, we have become an adjective in front of a category instead of creating new categories.

As the church, we create:

- Christian artists
- Christian companies
- Christian movies
- Christian music
- Christian politicians

You get the point.

We create "Christian" copycat versions of every main category out there. And when we do, more often than not, we produce something far inferior to the world's version.

Our movies have lower budgets than the average Hollywood film. We model our music after styles that are created by secular artists. Our businesses are less successful. The overall performance of the church seems to be far inferior to what "other nations" produce.

What is the key to seeing this change?

Kingdom culture!

We have to muster the courage to move away from established ways of doing things. We have to be willing to "forget" even the things that helped us see success in the past.

Again, what got us to where we are today, can't get us to where we are going!

Those who embrace the shift will find themselves in a conflict—a war between the house of Saul and the house of David.

THE ANATOMY OF A CULTURE

Once you see something, you cannot unsee it. So when you see catch a glimpse of a different future, it's hard to be satisfied with the current. It's both a blessing and a curse. I experienced this firsthand when I was watching TV years ago.

On the screen was a well-known television preacher talking about the kingdom of God. He was sharing principles, ideas, and stories to explain how it operates.

It was unusual for me to be watching Christian television; I don't really enjoy it very much and usually get bored pretty quickly. Yet, for some reason, that day I left the program on.

The preacher wasn't sharing much that I hadn't heard before. In fact, many of the illustrations he used were ones I had used myself in sermons many times.

Then, halfway into the broadcast, something supernatural happened. Something I had not experienced before. Something that ruined me in an instant.

As I was listening to the man talk about the kingdom of God, I suddenly SAW the kingdom of God. Somehow, what I knew about the kingdom became so real to me that I actually could SEE it. And when I saw it, it took a split second to ruin my belief system.

Everything I had ever known about God, church, ministry, and His kingdom was destroyed in a moment. I became aware that I knew *nothing*.

Why am I sharing this story?

Well, once I saw the kingdom of God, I knew that what I had been building was not that! I realized that if I were to pursue the kingdom as I had seen it, it would ultimately destroy the very things I had worked so hard for.

It took me several months to recover from that experience. I had nothing to say. Nothing to share. Nothing to preach. None of what I could come up with was significant enough to contribute to the conversation in context of what I now knew.

Frankly, I had what I can only describe as a personal faith crisis. I now knew something that I hadn't known before. I had seen something that I couldn't unsee. I had taken the "red pill" (for those who have watched *The Matrix* movies), and there was no way back.

How could I ever do anything that would be significant enough in context of what I had just seen?

The problem is that God will always be much, much bigger than what we can envision Him to be. The truth is that He will always be more glorious then what we can even begin to think or imagine.

Regardless of the level of revelation we might reach in our lifetime, He will always be far greater. There is nothing on earth that we can do or build for Him that will be able to contain His majesty in its fullness.

In a way, that sounds depressing, but it isn't. It is sobering, and we should be humbled by it. It is definitely a good process for everyone to go through; it just puts things in perspective. With this realization, one can look at the church and be relieved. We can look at Christianity and have hope.

The wisest man on earth, King Solomon, asked God a question in 2 Chronicles 6:18:

> *"But will God indeed dwell with men on the earth? Behold, heaven and the heaven of heavens cannot contain You. How much less this temple which I have built!"*

In his divinely apportioned wisdom, Solomon had come to realize that whatever he built for God on earth, it would not be able to contain Him who is seated in heaven. Not even the heaven of heavens could contain Him!

Yet, despite this conclusion, Solomon continued to build to the best of his ability. He brought sacrifices and praise unto the Lord until the house was finished. And God Almighty responded:

> *Then the Lord appeared to Solomon by night, and said to him: "I have heard your prayer, and have chosen this place for Myself as a house of sacrifice." —2 Chronicles 7:12*

God's glory came down in the temple that Solomon had built. The splendor of this temple didn't even come close to the splendor of Almighty God Himself. But Solomon had built it to the best of his ability, with the revelation he had. He did it with all his might and sacrificed unto the Lord continually. And as he did that, God responded.

Like Solomon, we have to strive for something greater and build to the best of our ability. When we do, God will respond.

When the dust of my faith-earthquake had settled, I realized that I had to make a decision to move away from previous mindsets, models, and ways of doing things and work toward shifting into a new paradigm that would allow me to be part of creating kingdom culture.

That is easier said than done. In most cases people would agree that kingdom culture is something that is needed. But I believe that often we don't understand the full impact of such a statement.

If we are truly going to shift our environment from a non-kingdom culture to a kingdom culture, the impact is going to be massive. This is not something that is easily done. You can't just say you "want kingdom culture" and expect it to happen without consequence.

The word "culture" is an exceptionally complex one—the second or third most complex word in the English language, it has been claimed.

Culture cannot be defined by one or two things. As a result, you can't just simply "change your culture" like changing a set of clothes.

Culture is created through the combination of a million little things like:

- Our values
- Our customs
- Our belief systems
- How we see ourselves
- How we see others
- What we eat
- How we eat it
- Our language(s)
- The way we dress
- How we pay taxes
- To whom we pay taxes
- Legislation
- Our form of government
- Our religion
- Our economy
- Family systems

And these just name a few!

Collectively, they create our whole way of life—our culture.

You can't just point to any one aspect and explain what culture is. It's everything. So by saying we are going to change culture, we're saying we're going to change EVERYTHING.

If we truly believe that—as God's people—we have to shift our culture to a kingdom culture, and if we're committed to the process, we're essentially saying that we're committed to changing everything we've ever done.

Are we really ready to go there? Because this rabbit hole may go much deeper than we wish.

Once we start shifting, it may unravel everything that is part of our current reality. However, at the same time, it's our only option if we're going to get to where God wants us to be.

Getting there will cost everything!

In the process we will need to be willing to change many things. Many things that are currently wrapped up in our existing culture but have to be redefined by true kingdom culture.

If you and I are going to be kings, we cannot govern from Shiloh. We cannot build our palace in Ramah. Those places are suffocating to kings.

Kingdom culture creates space to breathe. Kingdom culture promotes critical thinking. It allows you to create and do things you could never dream or imagine. Kingdom culture truly facilitates an environment for God's people where they can truly be kings.

Changing culture is hard. But it's also worth it.

CHAPTER SEVEN

GOD'S KINGDOM DICTIONARY: LEARNING TO SPEAK HIS LANGUAGE

G iven the future demands a complete culture shift, it's not possible to break down every aspect that needs to change in this book. However, I would like to explore a few big areas that will help us get our minds in the right place, so we can start processing the imminent shift we're facing.

When I say "big areas," I mean those that have a big-picture impact. For example, there are certain aspects of culture that are more based on preference that have little to no impact on the big picture. If you live in Africa, you may culturally be more inclined to eat mangoes as opposed to someone in Norway, where certain berries are preferred. Both are fruit. Both are tasty. However, there is no real impact when choosing one over the other.

Other cultural shifts will have a significant impact. Let's start with language.

Language is an extremely important part of every culture; if you don't understand a culture's language, it's going to be very hard to understand that culture at all. It has been said that a tourist is someone who laughs at everything but the jokes. In other words, tourists laugh because they don't understand— and they don't laugh because they don't understand!

Kingdom culture has its own language, and if we're going to understand kingdom culture, it's going to be crucial that we speak kingdom language. The problem is our religious baggage often stands in the way of truly understanding certain words.

The definitions of a lot of words we use in our religious church context have deviated from their original meanings over time. To understand kingdom language, we need to make sure we have a kingdom dictionary that defines the words that we use. That way we can get everyone on the same page.

For example, there is an old saying that Britain and America are "two nations divided by a common language." This tendency to use the same words but give them different meanings isn't limited to those two countries, however.

For almost three years, I lived in South Africa, where the main language is English. But just because they speak English doesn't mean the words they use mean the same things as they do here in the United States.

Take the word "costume." Here in the US we use that word during fall festivals or at Halloween when kids dress up as certain characters. They put on Spider Man or Star Wars costumes.

In South Africa, a "costume" is something you wear when you go swimming. People wear swimming costumes (bathing suits to Americans) when they jump into a pool. Same word. Same language. Totally different meaning.

So, one thing we need to make sure of as we shift culture is that we speak the same language.

THE LANGUAGE OF THE KINGDOM

In our church lingo, we use many terms that have lost their original meanings over the years. Words like church, testimony, witness, kingdom, nation, and elder name just a few.

Definitions always derive from the context in which the words are used, and God's context has always been about His kingdom. As we've learned, His primary agenda has always been for His kingdom to be administered by His people. The whole of Scripture is about that kingdom. Therefore, the big-picture context of anything in Scripture is that kingdom.

Knowing that everything God does and says is in the context of His kingdom, we know that any words He uses need to be interpreted in that light. The problem is that, historically, we've often not understood that context. Therefore certain words have developed a completely new meaning.

What does "kingdom" mean in Shiloh, for example? Shiloh was ruled by Eli the priest. It was not a kingdom. It didn't have a king. However, if your theology says that the word "kingdom" plays a crucial role in the expression of your faith, you're going to have to give that word meaning in the context of a non-kingdom environment.

To speak the language of the kingdom we have to go back to language school and redefine some words to recover their original meaning.

Take "church," for instance. Knowing that God's context for everything He does on earth is His kingdom, we need to recognize that the original definition of church was different than the one we have today.

It comes from the original Greek word *ekklesia*, which was not a new word that Jesus introduced. It already existed. *Ekklesia* was used by the Greeks to describe the public legislative assembly of the Athenians. Within the cultural context in which Jesus introduced church, people understood that He was referring to the political assembly of citizens of an ancient Greek state. In other words, *ekklesia* was a governmental term—not a religious one.

When Jesus used it to explain the kingdom, His audience knew that He wanted His people to organize themselves as a governmental entity. Not a religious entity!

What happens when you try to explain church in a non-kingdom environment? It's simple: It loses its original meaning. In fact, it develops a false definition. As a result, two people can use the same word and actually talk about two completely different things.

There are many, many other words with similar problems. When I speak about these things, I often lead a simple exercise that demonstrates my point. I ask the people in the room to remove their thinking from a religious context. "Don't think about church," I tell them. "Don't think about ministry. Don't think about the Bible. Move your thinking away from a religious place altogether."

Once everyone confirms they have done that, I ask them to give me definitions of certain words. For example, I ask if someone can give me a definition of the word "kingdom."

People will give me answers like this, "A kingdom is a country, state, or territory ruled by a king or queen."

However, when I ask the same question, but now in context of Scripture, I get a completely different definition. I get answers like, "Kingdom is a place where believers can all be equal," or, "Kingdom is a place where churches from different denominations can work together in a place of unity."

This exercise illustrates how our religious context has redefined terminology to fit our non-kingdom culture and therefore lost its original meaning.

The same happens with the word "testimony." Again, this is not a religious term; it's a legal term. As is the case with the word "witness."

Actually, many biblical terms are governmental and legislative in origin. Yet we've redefined them in the context of our religious culture.

The church of tomorrow needs to shift. This shift requires us to relearn an old language. We have to revisit some of our most basic terminology and develop kingdom definitions of these terms, so we can all be on the same page.

THE ECONOMY OF THE KINGDOM

I've had the privilege of traveling to forty or so nations in my lifetime so far and have lived for extended periods of time on three different continents. Having grown up in the Netherlands, I lived as a missionary in South Africa for almost three years, and have now been living in the United States since 2006.

Those experiences have underscored for me how important the economy of a nation is in creating the culture there. Each of the places I have lived has had a very different economy, which has had an impact on the culture. Not only have I used a different currency in each of these places, the trading power of each currency has been very different as well.

In South Africa, for example, we used the rand, which was incredibly unstable. Its value typically would fluctuate throughout the year and would always adjust based on "tourist season." It was ingrained in the culture that this would happen, and as a result, people would spend their money a certain way based on the value of the rand at certain times of the year.

Even what is displayed on the money is something that communicates what is important to the culture of each place. In the Netherlands, we had just transitioned from having famous Dutch historical leaders on our money (the Dutch guilder) to European Union-based visuals. The introduction of the euro had a true impact on the culture of the Netherlands and other countries that were part of the union.

In South Africa, the "big five" were displayed on our money, the five animals that are a proud part of South African culture: the elephant, the rhino, the lion, the leopard, and the African buffalo. Meanwhile, in the United States we display former presidents and leading political and historical figures.

Each of these countries also treats money differently. Based on their political structure, money "flows" differently in each place. The tax codes are different. The way the government deals with the taxes it collects is different.

All of that is to say that the economy of a nation has a major impact on the culture of a nation. So as we're changing culture from a "church culture" to a "kingdom culture," it should be no surprise that it's going to have an impact on the economy.

The economy of a kingdom is going to be different than the economy of a church. The economy of Jerusalem is going to look different than the economy of Shiloh or Ramah.

Why is this so important? Because the economy of a nation is its lifeblood. If the economy is healthy and money flows, the nation is going to flourish and be successful. Yet if the economy is stagnant, the whole nation is going to suffer as a result.

This is why "economic sanctions" are so powerful and effective. Back during apartheid, the world placed economic sanctions on South Africa. As a result, it didn't have the ability to trade with major parts of the world. There was a big impact on the economy, as well as the goods and services that people there had access to.

For example, when my family and I moved to South Africa in 2003, there were no Starbucks franchises in the country. Hard to imagine, right? It's different today, but back then the absence of certain international staples was the result of the economic sanctions placed on it by other nations.

When an economy is shut down, it shuts down a nation. Fund a nation, and you'll keep it alive.

Moving from a church culture to a kingdom culture, we are going to have to make a shift that is ultimately going to dry up the economy of what once was and exponentially multiply the economy that will be.

This sounds exciting—and it is—yet if we are not aware of what is going to be required, we may find ourselves holding the short end of the stick.

Like in the days of Joseph, who foresaw a rapidly changing economy, God wants to show us where we are going, so we can prepare ourselves now for what will be in the near future.

Let's go back to the history of David, and the economic shift that God declared through His prophets. Early on, during the rule of Eli, God prophesied through His servant that a massive economic shift was coming. He wanted the leadership in Shiloh to be aware so that they could prepare for what was about to happen.

We read about it in 1 Samuel 2:33-36. Speaking through a prophet, God says:

> *"And all the descendants of your house shall die in the flower of their age. Now this shall be a sign to you that will come upon your two sons, on Hophni and Phinehas: in one day they shall die, both of them. Then I will raise up for Myself a faithful priest who shall do according to what is in My heart and in My mind. I will build him a sure house, and he shall walk before My anointed forever. And it shall come to pass that everyone who is left in your house will come and bow down to him for a piece of silver and a morsel of bread, and say, Please, put me in one of the priestly positions, that I may eat a piece of bread."*

There is so much in these few verses to consider. Let's walk through them systematically.

A prophet showed up on Eli's doorstep one day and started to paint the picture of the future. He began by saying that *the descendants of your house shall die in the flower of their age.* In other words, he judged the house of Eli. Eli had had a great run. He wasn't an evil person, but ultimately he wasn't able to provide an environment that would allow Israel to be all that she could and should be. As we have already discovered, a priest-led government cannot administrate a kingdom. God basically thanked Eli for his service but announced that He was ready to move on to the next level. He announced that "the house of Eli" would have no place in the future government of Israel.

Then the prophet continued to declare that God would raise up for Himself *a faithful priest who shall do according to what is in My heart and in My mind. I will build him a sure house, and he shall walk before My anointed forever.* With the benefit of hindsight, we know that he was prophesying about the government of King David.

Even in the days of Eli, God declared prophetically that David's house would be established.

But here is the interesting thing: the prophet then started to explain the economic shift that was to take place between Eli's house and the house of David.

He said, *And it shall come to pass that everyone who is left in your house will come and bow down to him* [David] *for a piece of silver and a morsel of bread, and say, Please, put me in one of the priestly positions, that I may eat a piece of bread.*

The man of God prophetically declared that the economy of the house of Eli would dry up by the time the house of David was established.

Again, for us, Eli is not a person, he is a prophetic type of the church and the way we do church. God rejected the house of Eli and announced the rule of David. He basically said that whether you listened or not, sooner or later, the economy of the house of Eli was going to dry up completely. And if you did not align yourself with the house of David before that happened, all you could do was come to David and beg *put me in one of the priestly positions, that I may eat.*

Whether we want to accept it or not, the economy of God's kingdom is different than the economy of the church. In fact, it's much bigger. If you are dependent on the economy of the church to eat, then now is the time to start making adjustments because what feeds you today, can't feed you tomorrow!

Shiloh will ultimately experience economic sanctions because of its inability to operate as a kingdom.

With kingdom culture comes an economic shift that is going to impact the church as we know it in a very dramatic way. God wants us to see that, so we can reposition ourselves economically and become part of His new economy. And, believe me, it's going to be better than we had before!

As believers, we need to start investing in kingdom development rather than church. This type of giving will look radically different from how we've sown our money before. Don't be left as a descendant of Eli. You'll end up begging David for a job.

I know that money is a sensitive subject to many, but we need to recognize that a significant part of the conflict between the church of today and the church of tomorrow is about the economic shift that is slowly sucking the one dry while fueling the other to prosperity and growth.

Believe me, this shift is in everyone's advantage. God never replaces the old unless the glory of the new is greater (Haggai 2:9). What He rebuilds always transcends the limitations of what was torn down (John 2:19).

We may not know exactly what this shift will mean practically for church as we know it, yet one thing is for sure. It will demand from us the willingness to let go of traditional financial stability. A different type of economy is required to build a kingdom than is needed to sustain a church. Money will flow differently and end up in different places. Some of that may be unconventional or even controversial in the context of what we've always taught. Yet, let's be open for God to show us a higher way because there always is a higher way.

I'm talking about progressive revelation—revelation on the same subject matter that advances over time as God shows you additional dimensions.

For example, when it comes to finances, we often quote from the book of Malachi. We teach that biblical economics means we should be faithful in our tithes and offerings by quoting Malachi 3:8-10:

> "Will a man rob God? Yet you have robbed Me! But you say, 'In what way have we robbed You?' In tithes and offerings. You are cursed with a curse, for you have robbed Me, even this whole nation. Bring all the tithes into the storehouse, that there may be food in My house, and try Me now in this," says the Lord of hosts, "If I will not open for you the windows of heaven and pour out for you such blessing that there will not be room enough to receive it."

We can't rob God; we have to give! Our tithes and offerings are crucial in opening up the windows of heaven. Besides, we don't want to invite the devourer (Malachi 3:11) into our lives to keep us from being blessed by God.

There is truth in this that all believers have to understand, and when we do, we give, so we can keep the devourer from eating up our blessing. Then there is a higher understanding of the same thing. Yes, you definitely want to continue to give, but you start to understand that unless we come to the place of "death" in our giving, that the seed will not bear fruit. In John 12:24, Jesus puts it this way:

> *"Most assuredly, I say to you, unless a grain of wheat falls into the ground and dies, it remains alone; but if it dies, it produces much grain."*

We have a higher understanding on the same topic here. Sure, you want to give because you want the windows of heaven to open. You want to rebuke the devourer. That's all great. But now you're coming to see that none of this matters unless "the seed dies" first. Unless you come to the point where you truly understand that it's better to give than to receive regardless of the return, the seed will not render much grain. The seed you sow has to come to the place of death first before you see a harvest.

In other words, give regardless of the outcome. Even if your seed doesn't return a harvest, you still give. That's what it means to have the seed "die." When you give regardless of the return, it will truly die. And when the seed dies, it will produce much grain.

See: same subject matter, higher understanding and revelation.

But what if it doesn't stop there? What if there is yet a higher revelation about the same thing?

You gave simply because you didn't want to invite the devourer in your life. Then you realized that there was a higher understanding; giving in order to open up the windows of heaven appeared to only be the shallow end of the pool. Going deeper, you recognize that giving for the sake of giving causes the seed to die. It's better to give than to receive. Whether the windows open or not, you decide to give regardless.

But then comes a moment when you understood an even bigger truth about giving. Another dimension gets added to the same subject matter. Instead of waiting for the windows of heaven to open, you start to understand that, in fact, YOU are a window that God can choose to open and close to pour out blessings to others.

You understand that, wherever we are and wherever we go, we become windows at God's disposal. He can choose at any given time to use us to be a window of blessing. He can open us up or close us at His discretion. Why? Because we are blessed to be a blessing to others, in the spirit of how God called Abram to follow Him to a new place with the promise, "I will bless you and make your name great, so that you will be a blessing" (Genesis 12:2).

As Jesus said, "It is better to give than to receive" (Acts 20:35). We become windows that God can open and close to become a blessing to the world around us.

This is what I mean by progressive revelation. Just because you perceived at one point that you need to bring your *tithe to the storehouse* doesn't mean that there is nothing more to understand. God wants to provide us with revelation that will take us to another level. Revelation that will allow our minds to perceive a higher understanding of the same thing. Something that will redefine "storehouse" in a kingdom context.

Never settle when it comes to revelation. There is always something more to understand. There is always a higher way than how we have seen and done things historically. Even if we taught a certain thing for many years, it doesn't mean there isn't a greater reality.

This doesn't mean what we have taught was bad. It simply means that there is more to it than we could see before. So let's allow God to redefine our economy as we move into a kingdom context.

Like the prophet spoke to the house of Eli about a coming economic shift, He is speaking to the church today to give us an opportunity to be part of something bigger, something greater, and something far more prosperous than what we've ever been part of.

Let's shift!

CHAPTER EIGHT

A NEW KIND OF KINGDOM: A FAMILY, NOT AN INSTITUTION

God's agenda is to see His kingdom come on earth as it already is established in heaven, just as Jesus prayed. God prefers a monarchy over all other forms of government; His domain is to be governed as a kingdom. As His sons and daughters, we've been given the privilege of helping Him administrate this kingdom.

We need to remember that, just because God desires a kingdom, it doesn't mean He models it after the other kingdoms we see around us. God knows that His kingdom will provide His people with the best possible infrastructure, economic climate, and opportunities to succeed in life.

Now, a kingdom needs citizens, of course—people, a community that can benefit from living in that kingdom. And the main difference between the kingdom of God and other kingdoms is how it treats its citizens.

That's why the "kingdom message" is only complete in the context of a community. God has never wanted a kingdom for its own sake. That would be silly. He wants a kingdom that would serve a nation, a community of citizens. And He has wanted that all the way from the beginning: God created a domain where He placed man to rule and expand that domain. Part of the expansion was to multiply and populate that kingdom.

Even after the fall, God reintroduced that idea almost immediately. In Genesis 12:2, God speaks about His covenant with Abraham:

> "I will *make you a great nation; I will bless you And make your name great; And you shall be a blessing.*"

And in Exodus 19:6, we read how God told Moses to tell the people of Israel:

> "*And you shall be to Me a Kingdom of priests and a holy nation.*"

God wants two things. He wants a kingdom, and He wants a nation to both populate and administrate that kingdom. The one cannot exist with you the other. It's a package deal or no deal at all.

The kingdom God wants was designed to serve its people. A kingdom like the other nations will have its people serve the king and/or the organization.

See the difference?

In God's kingdom, the citizens also happen to be His children. This is another clear distinction in how the kingdom of God is different from any other kingdom around us.

In 2 Corinthians 12:14, Paul says, "For I do not seek yours, but you. For the children ought not to lay up for the parents, but the parents for the children."

Paul says it well: God didn't give us a kingdom to take from us, but He gave us a kingdom to add to us.

Samuel warns about the "symptoms" of having a king like the other nations:

> *Samuel told all the words of the Lord to the people who asked him for a king. And he said, "This will be the behavior*

of the king who will reign over you: He will take your
sons and appoint them for his own chariots and to be his
horsemen, and some will run before his chariots. He will
appoint captains over his thousands and captains over his
fifties, will set some to plow his ground and reap his harvest,
and some to make his weapons of war and equipment for
his chariots. He will take your daughters to be perfumers,
cooks, and bakers. And he will take the best of your fields,
your vineyards, and your olive groves, and give them to
his servants. He will take a tenth of your grain and your
vintage, and give it to his officers and servants. And he
will take your male servants, your female servants, your
finest young men, and your donkeys, and put them to his
work. He will take a tenth of your sheep. And you will be his
servants. And you will cry out in that day because of your
king whom you have chosen for yourselves, and the Lord
will not hear you in that day." —1 Samuel 8:10-18

What we see here is an inverted version of what God has in
mind for His people, His family. A kingdom like other nations
would have its citizens serve the "organization" as opposed
to the kingdom serving the nation that lives under the
administration.

God's kingdom was ultimately designed to serve us, its citizens. To set us up for success. To place us in an environment
like the Garden of Eden. A place of peace, harmony, authority,
and abundance.

God's kingdom today is the relaunch of His "Eden Project."

Yet in a kingdom like the other nations, you'll find yourself in a very different climate. Instead of having an environment created for your success, it demands its citizens bend over backwards to serve and sacrifice for the greater good of the organization and the king.

Now, of course, I understand that we serve the King (Jesus) and that we sacrifice whatever is needed to help build God's kingdom. But there is a clear distinction here. The wrong type of kingdom creates a high-pressure environment that manifests the type of side effects that Samuel talks about.

Proverbs 29:2 puts it this way:

> *When the righteous are in authority, the people rejoice; but when a wicked man rules, the people groan.*

God's kingdom should create an environment of happiness and rejoicing. A climate that creates space to breathe, live, and think for yourself. If you're in an environment where you feel spiritually suffocated and where your very best is never good enough, you should wonder if this is truly a place where God rules. If the spiritual climate that you're in doesn't facilitate room to think for yourself, you are probably in the wrong place.

Read through Samuel's side effects again, and see if you recognize any of them in your own life and the environment that you find yourself in. Do you ever feel like:

- The fruit of your labor is always being claimed to further someone else's agenda?
- The vision or the organization always trumps your dreams and desires?
- Your skills and gifts are assumed property of the commonwealth?
- Someone is always entitled to the best of your "field"?
- There is always pressure to give financially to the institution every time you see a harvest (or worse, even when there is no harvest)?

If so, you may be living under the wrong king because in God's kingdom, these side effects don't exist.

Now, please don't read into what I'm saying here. I do not mean that I am against tithing and sacrificial giving or that I don't want to use my gifting and success for the greater good. That is not what I'm talking about.

What I'm talking about is that the citizens of God's kingdom shouldn't experience being part of it a burden. In fact, they should reap the fruit of being part of such a kingdom daily. God's kingdom is one of righteousness, peace, and joy (Romans 14:7)!

Why? Because God's kingdom was designed to make you flourish and succeed. Not to control and to take from you. Being part of the kingdom of God should never be a burden to its citizens.

I remember teaching for a week at a Bible seminary. The school was part of an international ministry that was known to believe in kingdom culture. However, when I walked into the classroom I could just sense the opposite of what I believed to be the characteristics of what God's kingdom should manifest. I felt restricted, suffocated, and discouraged to think for myself.

The main clue that I was in a place that served the wrong kind of king was I noticed that the most committed people seemed to be the most unhappy, the least themselves, and the most uniform with everyone else who was also "highly committed."

When I started to teach about kingdom culture and referenced the byproducts and side effects of having the wrong kind of king, it didn't take long for people to start opening up about their unhappiness. And when one of the main leaders spoke to me in private about how he really felt (something he wasn't able to do in the culture he was part of) I knew that they were dealing with the wrong kingdom.

A HOLY NATION

Let's explore the word "nation." It is confusing—another of those terms that needs to be defined (or redefined) in context of kingdom culture. Our modern definition of nation has almost made it synonymous with the word "country." When we talk about "the nations of the world," our minds automatically visualize a map that defines the different countries and their geographic locations.

However, a nation is not a country. In fact, it has nothing to do with geography. A nation is not defined by a piece of land but rather by a group of people. According to the dictionary a nation is defined as "a large body of people united by common descent, history, culture, or language."

When God told Abraham and Moses that He wanted them to become nations, He had PEOPLE in mind. Not land. Now, of course He wanted (and even promised) His people some land, but that land was needed in order for God to *make them a great nation* and to *make their name great* so that they could *be a blessing*, according to His promise.

God wants a nation, and it's His good pleasure to provide it a kingdom.

The long war between the house of Saul and the house of David in part was a war between a house that served itself and a house that would serve a nation.

As God's nation, we are not a country. We are not defined by lines on a map or by the passport we carry. A nation is connected by blood. A nation is family.

That is, a nation, or a people, is born out of one person. The children of Israel were considered a nation because they were the seed of Abraham. They were his offspring. They had the same blood running through their veins. They were the same race. And so we see how God always works through lineage or family lines. He always works transgenerationally. He is not only the God of Abraham but the God of Abraham, Isaac, and Jacob.

Naturally speaking, whenever someone is born, they are always born as part of a people. Everyone is born into a lineage and is part of a nation. When you are born Dutch (like I was), you will stay Dutch forever. It is not your passport that defines the nation you are part of, but rather the blood that you received from your father. You may even live in another country or possess a different passport, but nothing will change the blood that flows through your veins. A nation is a nation because of the fact that everyone is kept together by a family relational network.

God has wanted a nation from the beginning: He has wanted a family!

He chose to give His family something called a kingdom and entrusted them to help Him govern it. God's kingdom is His family business. We run it together with Him.

The kingdoms of other nations don't operate that way. They don't run their domains as a family but rather suppress their citizens and place burdens on them to serve themselves.

God's kingdom is not an institution. It's a family. And He has decided to expand His rule through His children. Throughout Scripture, He has made it clear that this family structure is the foundation of how He's building this kingdom.

Jesus was very clear on this. He knew that there were two themes He needed to speak on consistently. You'll see them in all His preaching, teaching, and parables. Actually, He never really talked about any other topics.

These topics were "the kingdom of God" and "family." Read the Gospels: Everything Jesus ever shared was about God's kingdom and His father. He spoke about His family, and He spoke about the kingdom. That was it. I don't know where we started to put other things in Jesus' mouth, but He only spoke about these two things. When you read the Bible through that lens, it all is so clear.

The truth is that the whole Old Testament provides us with the ultimate blueprint for how God's people are connected and how they should organize themselves.

Why is this so important to understand? There are many reasons, but probably the most important one is that family defines us. It is our very identity.

In our non-kingdom culture, we may say that we're family, but in reality what defines us is the organization. Think about it. On a typical Sunday morning a pastor may "welcome the family to the house of the Lord." But are we really family?

If we truly believe that, then family is for life. It never changes. But in a non-kingdom culture, what defines you is the organization. Your membership to a certain congregation. The place where you worship. In a non-kingdom culture, a common question is, "Where do you go to church?" Your membership to a certain congregation is what defines you.

Then, when you move to another city or state, you find another "family" to be part of. This really proves that, even though we call something family, in reality it's the organization that defines us.

God has always wanted family. He has always wanted a nation. From the Garden of Eden all the way through to the book of

Revelation, we read and learn about God's relationship with His family and the nation that He chose to have a covenant with.

He placed men in the garden and mandated they multiply. He wanted a son to grow up and leave his father and his mother so that he could have his own family (Genesis 2:24). Even after the fall it was God's primary priority to reintroduce His desire to have a family when He promised Abraham that his descendants would be like the stars in the sky.

God's family on earth has always been God's priority. Throughout the Old Testament, we read the history of how God developed His family through Abraham, Isaac and Jacob, and ultimately how it grew to be a nation that consisted of twelve tribes.

Throughout the Bible, family wasn't defined by the organization the people were part of. It was defined by blood. That's why the book of Numbers has long chapters of genealogy that define each individual. It defines God's family tree.

Someone's identity in the Old Testament was defined by who they were related to.

The Bible doesn't talk about Joshua. It talks about Joshua, *son of Nun.*

It doesn't talk about David, but about David, *son of Jesse.*

In God's kingdom, family connects and defines us. Not organization.

Think about the Jewish people. They are scattered all over the world, yet they connect as a nation, a people. It's blood that connects and defines them. I'm partly Jewish myself, and I can't think of any synagogue that is famous because within Jewish culture it's never about the organization. The Jewish people's identity is not defined by the synagogue they are part of. It's the blood that runs through their veins. It doesn't matter where in the world they are, there is connection that is not defined by any organization that makes them one with other Jews.

If you're not connected by family, the only thing you can do to create a sense of unity is to develop an organization.

The prophet Malachi understood the importance of this. In fact, the last few verses in the Old Testament imply that moving into the New Testament time, God's people would at one point lose the revelation of being a nation, a family, resulting in a curse that would need to be broken.

In Malachi 4:5-6, the prophet declared:

> *"Behold, I will send you Elijah the prophet before the coming of the great and dreadful day of the Lord. And he will turn the hearts of the fathers to the children, and the hearts of the children to their fathers, lest I come and strike the earth with a curse."*

The earth is cursed without God's family; most problems in society are rooted in father issues. A whole book could be dedicated to this topic, but a lot of problems we encounter both in the world around us and in our own lives are the result of the lack of healthy family dynamics. The roots of crime, divorce, depression, dysfunction, and many other maladies oftentimes are the result of the lack of a healthy father in someone's life.

The church as we know it has learned to function as an organization. Not a family. As a result, we can never be a kingdom until the hearts of the fathers turn back to the hearts of the children.

Malachi's prophesy is a declaration of God's kingdom that will restore God's family in the earth. The war between the house of Saul and the house of David is in part about this restoration. The tension between the organizational church we know today and the organic family of God that He is restoring.

NEXT-GEN LEADERSHIP

It wasn't until David ascended to his throne that something remarkable happened, something significant that hadn't been possible prior to his kingship. None of the great leaders in the past had been able to do what David did.

What was that?

Transfer his rule down his lineage. Think about it: None of the leaders who preceded David were able to transfer their leadership position to the next generation within their family. The baton was always passed to someone who was non-family to the leader.

Moses, for example, passed the baton to Joshua who was actually from another tribe.

None of the judges passed the baton at all. In other words, their ministries died with them.

Eli's sons were corrupt.

Samuel's sons weren't much better.

And, as we have already noted, Saul's son, Jonathan, died with him in battle against the Philistines (even though he knew God's anointing was on David).

None of these leaders of old were able to transfer their leadership to their sons until David was king.

Jacob prophesied to his son, "The scepter shall not depart from Judah" (Genesis 49:10). Through these words God declared a few things that are important for us to understand.

First, we need to recognize that the only person who holds a scepter is a king. Even when Israel was just a small family, a clan, God already declared His kingdom through Jacob.

Second, Jacob prophesied about David. David was from the tribe of Judah, and he was the first true king of Israel.

Third, he also declared that the scepter would not *depart* from Judah, meaning that it would be passed on down through the generations. In other words, God declared His dynasty, His family of kings through David. Through David, the kingdom would be passed down through the generations, which in time would bring us Jesus, who ultimately birthed a new nation of kings—the church.

The kingship of David offers us a blueprint of what the church today should look like. A dynasty of royalty defined not through the name on the building but by family. A family that will not end through the death of a generation but that passes the baton through the generations effectively until God's kingdom is established on earth as it is in heaven.

PART THREE

A NEW PARADIGM:
MAKING
THE TRANSITION

CHAPTER NINE

THE KEY TO KINGDOM GROWTH: TEARING DOWN THE WALLS

In the second chapter of Zechariah, we encounter a man with a measuring line on his way to Jerusalem. He was passionate, full of zeal to build the city of God. He wanted to do the right thing and contribute to the strength and effectiveness of the city of God:

> Then I raised my eyes and looked, and behold, a man with a measuring line in his hand. So I said, "Where are you going?" And he said to me, "To measure Jerusalem, to see

what is its width and what is its length." And there was the
angel who talked with me, going out; and another angel
was coming out to meet him, who said to him, "Run, speak
to this young man, saying: 'Jerusalem shall be inhabited
as towns without walls, because of the multitude of men
and livestock in it. For I,' says the Lord, 'will be a wall of
fire all around her, and I will be the glory in her midst.'"
—*Zechariah 2:2-5*

This man's heart was in the right place. He loved the Lord, he was excited about the city of God, Jerusalem, and he was committed to giving his contribution to the building of that city. There seems to be nothing wrong with this picture, right? Just "another day at the office" for this man, happy to be about the work of the Lord, building the city of God.

Many of us are like this man. We're excited about and committed to the work of the ministry. We want to build the city of God. Our hearts are in the right place, and we can't wait to see that "city" completed, so it can become a blessing to many.

Yet there was more going on beneath the surface, a cause for concern. An angel appeared on the scene, and he abruptly stopped the man from what he was doing. He said, in effect: "What do you think you're doing? Don't you know that Jerusalem shall be inhabited as towns without walls?"

The angel made the man aware of something very important that changed everything in relation to the activity the man was planning. The angel pointed out to the man that Jerusalem, the city he was measuring and helping to build, wasn't going to have any walls.

What a game-changing revelation. Everything the man had done and everything he was planning to do had been based on the assumption that surely the city was going to have walls. His whole ministry had been founded on that assumption.

Yet, meanwhile, God had never intended Jerusalem to have any walls.

An awareness came to the man by supernatural intervention that changed his world forever. Remember, the primary tool this man had brought was a measuring line. He had specialized in using it. He was an expert at designing blueprints for building walled cities only to find out that the city he was trying to build was not going to have any walls whatsoever.

The very thing he had become excellent in had become irrelevant in context of this new information. He somehow had to unlearn the very thing he had studied all his life!

How do you measure a city without walls? How do you even plan to build a city without walls?

Basically, you don't.

Yet, God wants a wall-less city. God was making this man aware that what He is envisioning for the city is immeasurable!

God said to him: "Hey! Don't you know? I cannot be measured, and neither can the city that I'm building." He continued to explain to the man this city would have a multitude of people in it and that He Himself will be a wall of fire around them.

In other words, wherever the people of God are, that's where the wall will be. Not because we build it for God, but because God Himself will be it.

Amazing.

Think about this for a moment: What is a "measuring line"? Well, it's a tool that references a standard that once was created by man. Not by God, note, but by man. Somebody at some point in history decided that a foot was a foot. Where I'm from, the Netherlands, we use the metric system. We have meters. The thing about meters is that, at some point, someone (probably Mr. Meter?) decided that a meter was a meter. He set the standard right then and there.

From that point onward, anything that ever had to be measured was measured by that standard. Every measuring line created since has referenced that man's standard.

Could it be that we have measuring lines in our minds that reference a standard that was not meant to be a standard to begin with? Could it be that we are working on assumptions that need to be challenged? Could it be that God is trying to remove the measuring lines by which we measure our work?

So many times we have "strategic ministry" meetings to plan how we will grow what we are doing, and we set parameters for what it is going to look like. Yet God says, "I cannot be measured." You cannot design a wall-less city. In God's kingdom, each person is supposed to give birth to a uniquely unexpected expression of who God is. It cannot be measured. It cannot be planned.

Like the man with the measuring line, we need to be made aware of this, so we will cease putting effort into strengthening something that was never supposed to be built.

The bottom line: God's kingdom is fluid. It doesn't have walls. It flows with its people. Wherever they are is where His kingdom is.

An interesting concept, right? But it's the very opposite of how we do church. We build walls and point at what's inside of them, we give it a name, stick a logo on the building and call it church.

God's city, His kingdom, doesn't have walls. It's connected by blood. It's a family of people who collectively, through their efforts, administrate and establish God's kingdom.

"SPIRITUAL COMMUNISM"

The juxtaposition of those two words may have shocked you. After all, we know how communism denies the reality of God and stands in opposition to the freedom and fullness of the gospel. *What does human totalitarianism have to do with the spiritual,* you may be wondering?

Well, harsh as it may sound, I believe that much of the church as we know it today operates effectively as a "communist" entity. Please bear with me here! I'm in no way suggesting that it's the intent of our leaders to do so, but I want to suggest that a lack of kingdom culture pushes us subconsciously toward this kind of expression of what we believe.

Let me explain.

A communist government is one that owns all projects. In other words, everything belongs to the state. All initiatives are for the common good.

With that in mind, it's not too much of a stretch to see how the way we build churches unfortunately has many communist characteristics. As church leaders, we "plant churches" as walled cities. We pick a location, find a building, and give it a name.

Like a communist country, the government of our churches owns all projects. Ultimately the leaders control everything on the inside.

A typical church will have a variety of departments which its leadership controls:

- Children's Ministry
- Couples' Ministry
- Small Groups
- Sunday school
- Volunteers
- And so on.

If you are a member of the church and you have been proven faithful to the organization, you may be selected to be a leader within these departments. We call it "releasing people into ministry." This happens when you attend the meetings. When you volunteer your time. When you pay your tithes and give your offerings. Then you may be deemed worthy enough to be a leader within one of the "state's" departments.

Now, suppose you have a vision from God for a "clowning ministry." You talk to your pastor about your dream, and he says he's prayerfully going to consider adding such a department to the church's portfolio. A few board meetings later he has "good news": It's been decided to launch a clowning department in the church as an official ministry. And YOU are going to run it!

Now you start putting things in motion and you start clowning under the church's umbrella. But launching a clowning ministry turns out to be easier said than done. For a season of your life, you pour yourself into making this thing happen. Your time, energy, and money are being sown into what you know God is calling you to.

Finally there is a breakthrough. Things are starting to happen. Everything is going great. You are reaching people. People are offering to volunteer. You're building a small team. There is some real fruit as a result of the vision that had been burning in your heart for such a long time.

But then life happens. As a result, you are unable to attend church every Sunday. You have good reasons for your absence, but it's being frowned upon regardless.

Are you committed to this ministry or not?

Maybe you have skipped giving your tithe once or twice, also. Again, for good reasons. (I know, there should never be a good reason, right?)

What now?

More often than not, in our current church culture, you will be "released" from your position as a department leader. The department that was originally conceived by the vision you shared is now confiscated by the "government" and will be given to someone else.

Why? Because the organization "owns" all vision. It's the institution that controls all projects. Anything done outside of that structure is labeled as an independent initiative, maybe even dismissed as having "an Absalom spirit."

Now, let me repeat: I'm not saying any of our leaders intentionally set out to be "communist." But the wineskin we've utilized in our churches requires this type of behavior. It cannot produce anything else.

Like the man with the measuring line going to Jerusalem, we're assuming we need to have walls if we're building God's city.

The truth is that we can't administrate a kingdom from Shiloh. We can't be kings in Ramah. We have to shift to a place where kingdom culture can be the norm. A place where new wine-skins can be developed and where the vision belongs to the people, not "the state."

The kingdom of God is a free-market enterprise where the vision of the nation belongs to its people.

Acts 2:16-17 talks about what happens when God's Spirit is poured out on people:

> *But this is what was spoken by the prophet Joel: "And it shall come to pass in the last days, says God, That I will pour out of My Spirit on all flesh; Your sons and your daughters shall prophesy, Your young men shall see visions, Your old men shall dream dreams."*

When God pours out His Spirit in a place, something profound happens. Something more profound, more powerful than any miracle. Sure, God can heal the blind and raise the dead. He can make the lame walk and make the deaf hear. But when God pours out His Spirit on people, something far more powerful happens.

That old man who lost his dream a long time ago will dream again!

Those young men on whom the world looks down because "they will never accomplish anything" will receive a vision from God.

Those dreams and that vision manifested in the earth will expand the kingdom of God.

As we shift from church to kingdom culture, we as leaders will facilitate a spiritual climate that will allow God to pour out His Spirit on all people. As a result, the people, the nation, will own their vision, not the institution.

God's kingdom provides vision and dreams for its people. It's that vision and those dreams that expand and increase His kingdom. The people of God's kingdom own the vision of the kingdom. Not just some select individuals, but "all flesh" will have dreams.

This is important to understand because it requires a completely different type of government to facilitate an environment that will do that. It cannot happen in Shiloh or Ramah. Everything will need to be shifted.

WALLING A CITY VS. ADMINISTRATING A KINGDOM

Historically, we've built the church as a walled structure not because we've had our hearts in the wrong place, but mostly because we haven't known any better. We grew up in Shiloh and Ramah and didn't have a point of reference for a kingdom. We grew up under priests and prophets and, in some cases, a king like other nations. We never really experienced a true kingdom culture.

How do you administrate and develop a kingdom? Not by doing what we've always done. A kingdom is never expanded by building walls. In fact, we have to tear down the walls we've built in the past in order to see His domain increase.

Kingdom expansion doesn't happen through institution and/ or control. It happens through empowering people to live their dreams.

Conceptually, most ministry leaders would agree with that statement, but on a practical level we're so accustomed to the old wineskin that by default we tend to create a culture of control. It's called muscle memory. We simply don't have any other point of reference for any other form of government.

If we're truly going to see a kingdom culture shift, it's going to require a completely different type of government. One that is going to revolutionize the way we do church. A culture that by default cannot do anything but tear down walls and break control. We don't "declare war" on the way things are, but the emerging kingdom culture will cause conflict by its very nature. And as a result, the walls will come down.

So what is the difference between building a walled city and administering a kingdom? To get an idea, take your mind back four hundred years to when the Pilgrims landed the Mayflower at Plymouth Rock.

The people on board were delegates of the king of England. They had been sent by the monarch to expand the kingdom, the commonwealth of England.

When they arrived, they came into uncharted territory. The story of the Mayflower is the origin story of what is now called the United States. The time between 1620 and today tells the story of how this new world was developed.

Isn't it amazing what has happened in just a little over four centuries?

So much has been developed in such a relatively short period of time. How is that even possible? Well, the main reason is because of the way the government of the kingdom of England operated. It didn't send people to land in Massachusetts and set up a walled structure, give it a name, and invite those around to join "the city." The people's mindset was completely different.

They planted the flag of England when they landed and declared that this new land was now property of the king. They set up a headquarters which became the governmental administration of the kingdom rather than its center. Out of that, all activity was administrated. This is very different than having a center within which all activity happens.

Then the territory expanded as a result of the vision of the people, not the institution.

One person wanted to start a bakery. Another became a butcher. Others got involved in farming and manufacturing. The cumulative efforts of all the citizens resulted in the expansion of that kingdom. It was not controlled by a walled structure, but rather developed by the empowerment of the people to live the dreams that were in their hearts.

Now, think about a city like New York. Nobody planned it. The city became a city because the people who were there at one point had a dream, a vision for a specific thing they wanted to do in their lifetime. By acting upon that vision and through the manifestation of those dreams, the city became what it is today.

Nobody is in charge of the city. Nobody controls it. Yet collectively it's property of the nation.

Sure, there is law and order, ordinances and rules, but there is no one entity that controls or owns every initiative in New

York. The city became the city it is today because of the manifestation of the dreams of the people who live in it.

This is the difference between a walled city and what I just described. It requires a different type of government, a completely different way of thinking. If we're going to adopt kingdom thinking into our church culture, it's going to demand a complete paradigm shift for us as leaders. Something that by default will completely tear down the structures we've built and redefine everything we know about how to "do church."

The problem with walled cities is that they can't grow because they are limited by their walls. Back in the Netherlands, where I grew up, our cities historically were walled, or in some cases they had canals around the city center. Everything happened within those limits; life flourished. However, once a city reached its capacity, it would have to be expanded.

The only way this could happen was by building a new wall that extended the perimeter or by digging a new canal to accomplish the same objective. Yes, the city was expanded for growth by doing these things, but a lot of effort was put into creating what became just the next limitation. The new wall became another limitation. The new canal defined the next restriction the city would be conditioned to. All the time, energy, and money poured into this new wall would create marginal increase in capacity. The ROI was simply not there.

That's how we have built churches historically. We put up a building and "bring people in" until we reach capacity. Then we launch a capital campaign to build a slightly larger building to accommodate the growth.

I have to be honest with you: this depresses me. Even the thought of building and leading a 20,000-strong church feels so small to me in a kingdom context. You can't build a city that way, let alone a kingdom. It's the wrong paradigm.

In context of kingdom culture, even a 20,000-member church is thinking too small. Not because we want to create "bigger churches," but because a kingdom culture and administration will potentially develop something far greater than a large organization.

We need a leadership, a form of government, that will allow us to live our dreams and to own our visions so that in a very short time we can see a lot of growth and advancement. Multiplication can't happen in a city with walls. Multiplication happens when we allow each citizen of the kingdom to live his or her dream.

CHAPTER TEN

A NEW HORIZON: LOOKING AT CHURCH DIFFERENTLY

L et me continue to illustrate the difference between what we traditionally have done to develop churches and what the administration of a kingdom looks like by sharing an experience that dates back to when I was a teenager, living in a discipleship home owned by the church I was part of at the time.

A good friend who was one of the ten guys living there shared a vision he had.

In it, he saw what he described as a Colosseum-like stadium. It had five levels on the inside where people could sit and watch what was going on down in the center. The structure of the five levels represented the five-fold ministries Paul writes of in Ephesians 4 (apostles, prophets, evangelists, pastors, teachers). They provided structure for the masses to be equipped inside of the arena, where from time to time there would be entertainment.

A gladiator would show up in the central arena to fight, and all would cheer him on. There was excitement and noise as the gladiator would face and overcome his opponent. The gladiators were heroes for fighting the battles. They were the center of activity. They were the VIPs, the celebrities that everyone else wanted to be like. People would dream that, one day, maybe they could become a gladiator. It was the ultimate calling.

Then the scene changed for my friend. It was as if the arena was flipped inside-out. Now the five levels faced outward, and the people who had previously seen looking down at the gladiator in their center were now gazing out toward the horizon where the sky met the land in the distance.

The gladiator was still on the inside, but nobody was watching him anymore because their outlook had changed. Their paradigm had been completely altered. The possibilities of what they could envision for their lives had expanded from becoming a gladiator one day to basically whatever they wanted to be. The structure of the "five-fold ministry" was still there, but it was oriented in a new way. They were pushing people out, instead of pulling people in.

My friend's vision reminded me of the illustrations you see of the people of Israel encamped in the wilderness. They have God and the tabernacle on the inside with the twelve tribes encamped around it. They are set up for growth. There is nothing constraining, nothing to keep them from expanding. They are connected to the core, yet they are free to expand into the horizon.

The vision my friend shared that day perfectly defines the shift that we're currently going through. We're going from an outside-in model (church) to an inside-out model (kingdom).

The only way the inside-out kingdom model is going to work is if a new generation of leaders can fully embrace kingdom culture. A domain that will have an environment and climate where its citizens will have dreams and visions for their own lives. A kingdom environment that will have no limitations for its citizens, and therefore no limits to the increase of the kingdom itself, either.

Living water is not meant to be bottled!

Let me explain that statement. It adds another visual to what it means to shift to kingdom culture.

What is the shape of water? Well, it depends, doesn't it? The shape of water is controlled by the shape and size of the container that it is poured into. For example, when water is poured into a glass, the shape of the water takes on the shape of the glass in which it now resides. In fact, it is scientifically impossible for water to take on any other shape than the shape of its container.

Yet water has the unique property to seep into any crack and any corner of a space, if we allow it to do what it does naturally. When we let water do whatever it wants, it has an incredible ability to touch places that can't be touched by anything else.

Water is a metaphor used throughout the Bible, which reflects the reality that it is the greatest asset God has entrusted us with to bring life to the world around us. There are more than one hundred scriptures that talk about the "living water" that God gives us as believers. This living water has the ability to reach every corner of society if we allow it to do what it naturally does. That is, unless we put this water into a shape that limits it from reaching the corners of the earth. Like a "walled city."

Could it be that we as church leaders have created systems and structures in our ministries that have become a container that limits the shape of water, so it can only exist within the shape of our organizations?

Could it be that we have turned our greatest asset (living water) into a non-liquid asset, keeping it from being exchanged on the open market? In the business world, both liquid as well as non-liquid assets can have tremendous value. However, the full value of a non-liquid asset is not accessible if we want to use it now.

Some of the cities in our country that have the highest number of churches per capita seem to struggle the most with poverty, crime, and violence. Somehow, our greatest asset isn't liquid enough to seep into the cracks of society and fix our most basic problems.

As I have considered these issues, I have come to the conclusion that we often limit the shape of the living water we've been entrusted with to the four walls of our ministries simply because of wrong assumptions we've adopted as truth. We've been called to reshape water and "liquidize" this asset so that we can truly touch culture and impact our society. To do so, we have to unlearn some basic "truths" that keep us from being effective as the church.

There are a couple of concepts that have helped me become a more 'liquid leader." I share them in the hope they will help you reshape the water you carry in the same way they have helped me.

In the New Testament, many of the stories Jesus shared were intended to correct our misconceptions. For example, in Matthew 13, we read the well-known parable of the wheat and the tares. The danger of passages like this is that, because we know them so well, we assume we've learned all we can learn. One area that this parable addresses is the tendency to separate ourselves from the world around us.

> *Jesus told them another parable: "The kingdom of heaven is like a man who sowed good seed in his field. But while everyone was sleeping, his enemy came and sowed weeds among the wheat, and went away. When the wheat sprouted and formed heads, then the weeds also appeared. The owner's servants came to him and said, 'Sir, didn't you sow good seed in your field? Where then did the weeds come from?' 'An enemy did this,' he replied. The servants asked him, 'Do you want us to go and pull them up?' 'No,' he answered, 'because while you are pulling the weeds, you may uproot the wheat with them. Let both grow together until the harvest.'"* —Matthew 13:24-30

The servants of the man in the story (us) had the tendency to separate the tares from the wheat that had been sown in the same field. Jesus later explains that "the field is the world"

(v. 38). Guess what? In order to reach the world, we have to be in the world. And guess what else? There are going to be "tares" growing among us.

Instead of trying to separate and isolate ourselves from the tares, we need to allow ourselves to grow where we are planted. Let both grow together until there is a harvest!

Which brings me to the second point. As a kid, I always liked to look at those big maps that tracked the apostle Paul's travels as he preached the gospel in all corners of the earth. Each journey of Paul was identified by a dotted line that stretched from country to country and city to city.

It wasn't until many years later that I realized that these dotted lines were not the same ones that you would see if you were trying to pick your favorite cruise vacation on a travel website. Paul's dotted lines were in fact trade routes. He didn't join a group of tourists on a big recreational boat. He boarded merchant ships that took him from point A to point B.

The truth is that the gospel has always traveled through trade!

Trade happens in every sphere and segment of society. By allowing it to become the infrastructure and distribution model for the kingdom, we will be able to reach every corner of our communities organically. Understanding this causes us to rethink the way we lead our churches.

Ninety-eight percent of all people in church are not working for the church. Most Christians have jobs in the market-place, by which I'm not referring only to traditional business. I'm talking about every form of trade that creates culture, including sports, arts, entertainment, politics, education and much more. As church leaders, we need to learn to leverage the fact that our people are already living and working "in all corners of the earth." By allowing them to grow where they are planted, we will reshape water to reach those corners until we see a harvest.

Yet, most of our efforts are geared toward initiatives that strengthen the status quo and that keep our greatest asset non-liquid. We don't need another new program or project to "reach the world." All we need to do is tear down the walls that limit the shape of water and allow it to flow into places where it experiences the least resistance.

As we already learned from Zechariah 2 a town without walls cannot be measured! What God wants to build cannot be measured.

The city of God is fluid. It's liquid. Let's be liquid leaders and help reshape water in our lifetime!

THE KINGDOM OF GOD
IS LIKE FACEBOOK

Some years ago, I traveled back to the Netherlands to minister. I was on my way to a very small home church in the east of the country when the Holy Spirit gave me a parable.

He said to me, *The Kingdom of God is like Facebook.*

At first I thought this was kind of a weird statement. What did Facebook have to do with the kingdom of God? It didn't make sense.

At the time Facebook had been around for a while and was experiencing rapid, explosive growth around the world. It hadn't been growing incrementally; it had been multiplying exponentially in a very short period of time.

As I was thinking and praying through this statement, God started to show me the parallels between Facebook and His kingdom: Facebook is a domain to which everyone is invited. Just as all are welcome in God's kingdom, everyone is welcome to join the Facebook domain.

But just because someone is invited doesn't mean they can enter any way they want. There is still protocol, a "legal way" to enter the domain. Even though some couples have a joint Facebook account, officially you're not allowed to piggyback on someone else's access. The domain is designed for individual access by following certain steps.

Once you enter the Facebook world, there are rules, protocols, and ethics that need to be followed. For example, you can't just use your access to abuse your relationships and target their friends to sell them on your multilevel marketing scheme. Once the Facebook algorithms pick up on such abuse, you will be "blocked" or temporarily suspended from certain activities.

Nor can you use someone else's identity—their picture or email address—to get into the domain. Your identity will need to be verified before you can start operating in the "Facebook kingdom."

So, yes, there is "law and order" within the domain, to a certain extent. However, once you are in the Facebook ecosystem there is a tremendous freedom to be who you want to be. You are able to express yourself however you want. You can post your pictures. You can like what you want to like, and you can consume whatever content you want to consume.

You can also develop your own friends circle however you would like to. Nobody forces you to be friends with certain people. It's up to you to build your own community. In fact, as a result of this principle, no identical circle of friends to the one you have around your profile exists.

If you have vision for something, you can start your own group or page and invite whoever you want. And they can decide whether or not they want to join or follow your initiative. There are no hard feelings if someone doesn't join your group. It's totally up to the individuals to express themselves how they want to within the boundaries of the Facebook ecosystem. As a result, no profile is the same. Everyone's expression within the domain is completely unique.

Maybe as church leaders we should learn from this. I sure did as I was pondering this parable. I started to realize that in our traditional church culture we tend to develop an atmosphere that by default demands the opposite of what I just described.

The more "in" someone is with the vision of our church, the more uniform this person seems to become with everyone else who is also "in." The more committed someone is to a ministry, the more their community and circle of friends starts to become identical with everyone else who is highly committed to that vision.

As highly committed church members, we seem more likely to be involved in the same activities as everyone else who is highly committed. The culture we—often unintentionally—develop pushes people to do the same things, with the same people, at the same time. We pray on Monday. On Tuesday we have Bible study. On Wednesday there are small groups. And so on. Before long, we start talking the same, acting the same, dressing the same, and behaving the same as everyone else within our little walled city.

The more "in" and "sold out" we are, the more we start to look and behave like everyone else who is "in" and "sold out."

This is the opposite of the culture of God's kingdom. In His kingdom, each individual is pushed into authenticity and personal identity. Yes, like Facebook, the domain of God's kingdom is what makes us one. But within the kingdom, there is so much space. There are no walls. Its territory stretches around the globe.

It's a safe place to become whoever God wants you to be.

CHAPTER ELEVEN

SACRIFICE OVER EXCELLENCE: THE HEART OF CHANGE

When I talk about inside-out thinking to any group of ministry leaders, they will almost always conceptually agree with what I'm sharing. But just agreeing with this paradigm is not enough. It demands of us a massive shift. A shift that is symbolically and prophetically communicated to us through David moving to Jerusalem.

He knew that the historic "capitals" of Israel were not going to be the place from which to run a kingdom. Shiloh and Ramah weren't suitable for kings. He had to move to a new place. And when he did, he became successful everywhere he went.

Personally I'm in an interesting position. On the one hand, I am a ministry leader, yet on the other I'm a businessman and marketplace leader. I run multiple companies, and in fact most of my time is spent in the business world.

I was talking to a friend the other day who is in a similar position. We connected because we are sort of an anomaly. He was telling me the story how 15-20 years ago, focusing on business was oftentimes frowned upon by ministry leaders. It was almost perceived as a distraction from what really mattered: Why would you focus on business and making money if you knew that God had called you?

I remember similar dynamics, how I was discouraged from engaging in business. God had called me to ministry, and I should just trust Him to take care of me, I was told. No need to be "in the world." Being in business was perceived as wrong. It was simply not church-centric enough.

We have come a long way in just a decade. This dualistic approach is something that is now rejected by most modern-day ministry leaders. The center of church is shifting from a traditional church view to a kingdom view. And to be part of this shift we have to pack our bags and leave Shiloh.

While most church leaders these days have embraced the idea that there is such a thing as "kingdom business," they fail to understand that "the church in the marketplace" cannot operate out of Shiloh. No kingdom business can be done there, or in a Ramah environment.

But here is the kicker. No kingdom *ministry* can be done in Shiloh or Ramah, either. Both have to shift. Both marketplace leaders as well as ministry leaders have to shift to a new place where they can finally coexist.

"Jerusalem" is the only place where ministry and marketplace can collaborate.

If we as ministry leaders truly want to collaborate with marketplace leaders, it's going to require a radical shift from both parties. Neither should exist in merely a church culture. Both will need to move away radically from existing paradigms and adopt kingdom culture if we're truly going to be in a place where we can coexist.

"The house of David" is destined to create that environment and help us migrate to Jerusalem—a place from where God's kingdom can be administrated. A place that doesn't only have an outside-in leadership model, but also rules from a place where old wineskins have been completely abandoned.

Let's look at David's shift a little closer. He had his priorities straight. The first thing he did was to make sure the ark of the covenant was part of the journey—something that Saul never did. David collected the ark from the house of Abinadab where it had been for over twenty years. We should learn from this: David knew he needed to make sure that the presence of God was part of his journey.

This didn't happen without mistakes, however. Not unexpected, given that David had no point of reference for what he was doing. On some level, he was just "winging it." Other than Saul, David had no example of anyone who had gone before him. And Saul certainly wasn't a role model that he wanted to emulate.

In 2 Samuel 6:3-15 we read about the mistake that David made as king:

> So they set the ark of God on a new cart, and brought it out of the house of Abinadab, which was on the hill; and Uzzah and Ahio, the sons of Abinadab, drove the new cart. And they brought it out of the house of Abinadab, which was on the hill, accompanying the ark of God; and Ahio went before the ark. Then David and all the house of Israel played music before the Lord and all kinds of instruments of fir wood, on harps, on stringed instruments, on tambourines, on sistrums, and on cymbals.
>
> And when they came to Nachon's threshing floor, Uzzah put out his hand to the ark of God and took hold of it, for

the oxen stumbled. Then the anger of the Lord was aroused against Uzzah, and God struck him there for his error; and he died there by the ark of God. And David became angry because of the Lord's outbreak against Uzzah; and he called the name of the place Perez Uzzah to this day.

David was afraid of the Lord that day; and he said, "How can the ark of the Lord come to me?" So David would not move the ark of the Lord with him into the City of David; but David took it aside into the house of Odeb-Edom the Gittite. The ark of the Lord remained in the house of Obed-Edom the Gittite three months. And the Lord blessed Obed-Edom and all his household.

Now it was told King David, saying, "The Lord has blessed the house of Odeb-Edom and all that belongs to him, because of the ark of God." So David went and brought up the ark of God from the house of Obed-Edom to the City of David with gladness. And so it was, when those bearing the ark of the Lord had gone six paces, that he sacrificed oxen and fatted sheep. Then David danced before the Lord with all his might; and David was wearing a linen ephod. So David and all the house of Israel brought up the ark of the Lord with shouting and with the sound of the trumpet.

There is so much to take to heart from this event. Let's try to unpack it.

RIGHT, NOT NEW

First, we see that David was committed to "shift." He knew he couldn't stay where the generations that had preceded him had governed from. He had to set up shop somewhere else. And so on to the City of David, Jerusalem, he was.

The mistake he made, though, was in putting Uzzah in charge. Not that Uzzah was a bad guy; I'm sure he was a good individual. He had clearly gained David's trust and respect over the years, to the point where the king wanted him to be the guy who was in charge of the big move.

Largely, Uzzah has through the years been painted as this guy who didn't know what he was doing. The guy who screwed up. He has been villainized in many sermons as the man who train-wrecked David's first project as king.

But I have a lot of sympathy for him.

Think about it. Uzzah didn't have a point of reference for a true kingdom. The only king he had known was Saul, and he hadn't offered any mentorship on to handle the ark of the covenant. In fact, the only point of reference that Uzzah had was really how Israel's enemy, the Philistines, had treated the ark.

What did they do? Well, after capturing the ark from Eli and his sons, the Philistines ultimately returned it to Israel after they were struck by plagues. They decided that it was a bad idea to keep possession of the ark because it was bad luck for them.

In 1 Samuel 6:7, we read what the Philistines' spiritual leaders counseled:

> *"Now therefore, make a new cart, take two milk cows which have never been yoked, and hitch the cows to the cart; and take their calves home, away from them. Then take the ark of the Lord and set it on the cart."*

Samuel was at the helm in this moment when God's ark was returned to where it belonged. For several decades this story echoed throughout Israel, making sure that everyone knew about the day that this miracle happened.

So when it became time for Uzzah to coordinate the next shift, it only made sense to him to use the same method. It had been done before, so why not do it again that way? Why fix it, if it ain't broke?

Uzzah simply adopted what had been successful in the past.

Big mistake! But who could blame him?

The resulting events even confused David to the point where he was both ANGRY as well as AFRAID of what had just happened.

If this was what it was going to be like, he wasn't sure if it was what he wanted anymore. He spiraled down emotionally to the point where he was simply not sure if he was still "in." He needed a break. Time to think. Was this shift really God? How could it be, if it resulted in the death of one of his most trusted delegates?

It was all very confusing. What had he done wrong?

David had put the ark on a new cart, just as had been done successfully before. Then he made sure there was an atmosphere of worship. He made sure there was music before the Lord, with all kinds of instruments of fir wood, harps, stringed instruments, tambourines, sistrums, and cymbals. He gathered the best of the best for his worship team.

So what in the world could he have possibly done wrong to deserve what had happened? This simply wasn't what he had signed up for! Sure, he accepted the job offer when Samuel showed up that day to anoint the next king of Israel, but this was not part of the job description given to him.

Needing time to think, David aborted the mission and decided to take a three-month sabbatical.

He took the ark aside, into the house of Obed-Edom. But then something interesting happened. The Lord remained in the house of Obed-Edom those three months. And the Lord blessed Odeb-Edom and all his household.

Remarkable. The same presence that had killed Uzzah now blessed Obed-Edom and all those who were in his house.

That must have been even more confusing. Yet, at the same time, it released a sense of hope—hope that he hadn't been wrong completely. Maybe David had just been missing a certain detail that was important to understand.

One thing had become clear to him during his sabbatical: The ark of God had the ability to bless as much as it had the ability to curse if it was mistreated. This understanding put him on a path that took him to a place of confidence needed to make the decision to try again.

David's conclusion was that what had worked for the Philistines was probably not the model that he wanted to adopt. When the was ark returned back in Samuel's days, it was merely a restoration of what had been lost, rather than something new that would move God's people forward into His eternal intent for mankind. It was a "model" of something that was done, and tolerated by God, for whatever reason, when followed by the Philistines, Israel's enemy.

David started to understand that the past could not be repeated. This time it had to be done differently.

It wasn't about the worship team.

It wasn't about the new cart.

Being "new" wasn't the only criteria. It also had to be done "right."

You see, the ark was never meant to be carried by a cart—treated as a part of a system to be followed—but rather by the priests that God had called to carry it all along. The presence and government of God was meant to be carried on the shoulders of the Levites (Deuteronomy 31:9).

IT COSTS EVERYTHING

During his timeout, David realized that he shouldn't just look at current "church history" and deduce strategy for the future. No, he had to look at the big picture and listen to what God had declared from the beginning.

As he was pondering how to do it differently, he gathered the courage to try again—with some important adjustments.

This second time there was no man-made cart involved. Instead, David put Levites in charge of carrying the ark on their shoulders.

The second thing he did was to downgrade his ministry team. No more stringed instruments, tambourines, and cymbals. Sure, music played a role, but it wasn't going to be the same as before. The sound of the trumpet was enough this time. Pretty bare bones, but David had started to understand it wasn't about "the show."

It had become all about the sacrifice. As we read earlier in 2 Samuel 6:13-14:

> And so it was, when those bearing the ark of the Lord had gone six paces, that he sacrificed oxen and fatted sheep. Then David danced before the Lord with all his might.

Picture that. All the way from the house of Obed-Edom to Jerusalem, every six feet, David sacrificed oxen and fatted sheep. That's plural. So at the very least two oxen and two sheep were sacrificed every six feet.

According to some experts, it was around ten miles from Obed-Edom's house to Jerusalem. That means David would have stopped at least 7,500 times to sacrifice at least four animals. That's thirty thousand animals at the very least.

Think not just about the number of animals, but also the time it took to go through the ceremony of doing so. All while dancing with all one's might!

The lesson here is one of sacrifice. Our worship team can't compensate. The shift between "church" and "kingdom" requires a lot more. It's a shift that will cost us everything. It demands that we leave behind the things of old. The things that have worked in the past. Trying to shortcut the process by doing it any other way will cost us greatly.

In Daniel 2:44, the prophet speaks of God establishing a kingdom "which shall never be destroyed; and the kingdom shall not be left to other people; it shall break in pieces and consume all these kingdoms, and it shall stand forever."

In Luke 20, Jesus told the parable of the people who mistreated those a vineyard owner sent to check on it, even killing the man's son. In verses 17-18 we read:

> *Then He looked at them and said, "What then is this that is written: 'The stone which the builders rejected has become the chief cornerstone'? Whoever falls on that stone will be broken; but on whomever it falls, it will grind him to powder."*

The rock of that kingdom is either going to fall on us, or we are going to fall on it. Either way it's going to hurt! It's the difference between being broken by it and being crushed by it.

Uzzah died trying to do it the traditional way. Uzzah's story offers us an example of what not to do. We can't make the same mistake.

What God demands from us is EVERYTHING.

We can't just bring out the smoke machines and do things the way we've always done them. Excellence isn't what is going to get us to Jerusalem. It's going to take sacrifice and complete surrender.

David danced in his ephod; he was willing to strip down and become a priest in the presence of the King of kings. Yes, he was the true king of Israel, but ultimately he was willing to lay down his own kingship—which qualified him to become that man after God's own heart.

No, David never became perfect, yet he became the king, the first true king of Israel. The one king whose scepter didn't depart from his house. His kingship was passed down the generations all the way through Jesus, to us.

We need to pick up that scepter to rule once again, and bring kingdom culture back in the manner that David modeled for us. No, it won't come cheap. It will not be done easily. It will require great sacrifice, and the willingness to cast down our crowns to the point where we will wear only a linen ephod.

But the reward is great. Let's leave Shiloh. Let's move away from Ramah.

Jerusalem, here we come!

CHAPTER TWELVE

TRAINING FOR REIGNING: THE HARD PATH TO KINGSHIP

The conflict we find ourselves in is inevitable. It's not a war that we declare; it's one we've stumbled into. As God advances His kingdom in the earth, those who align themselves with what He is doing will find themselves in conflict with the past.

The battle between the house of Saul and the house of David was the result of God sticking to His original plan, which was to deliver to His people a kingdom. Not a kingdom like the other nations, but a kingdom that would provide an environment for His people to prosper on the earth.

Saul was the manifestation of the desire for a king like the other nations. A king that would, by default, manifest symptoms counterproductive to what God had in mind for His people.

In a way, Saul was set up for failure. He didn't even want the job in the first place, and when he got it he failed to shift. He became a KINO, king in name only, who ruled from a place in the past. Anointed king in Ramah, the city of Samuel, and appointed in Mizpah, one of Samuel's "campuses," Saul then returned to his home in Gibeah. There was no progress beyond what he had inherited from the past.

Saul was a king, but the characteristics of the kingdom he ruled were not the characteristics of God's kingdom. Yet the talk of the town was that God had given His people a kingdom. The "kingdom message" had become the current message among God's people. Yet the kingdom that manifested itself was nothing like God's true kingdom.

That must have been confusing. The prophets had spoken about a kingdom. Now they had anointed and appointed a king to be a leader in that kingdom, yet it wasn't the type that God had in mind when He created the heavens and the earth.

When things are defined as something they are not, it creates confusion. Let's look at some of the core differences between

Saul's kingdom and David's kingdom, between what they were and what they should have been. They illustrate the kind of kingdom we're dealing with.

HEAD AND SHOULDERS HIGHER

When Saul is first introduced in 1 Samuel 9:2, he is described as follows:

> *There was not a more handsome person than he among the children of Israel. From his shoulders upward he was taller than any of the people.*

Saul was "Mr. Israel," the best-looking guy in the nation. Not only was he attractive, he was also the tallest man around. As a matter of fact, he was head and shoulders above everyone else. His physical appearance symbolically communicated his authoritarian regime, which he ended up calling a kingdom.

Saul's house operates through a leadership model where the main leader is just a little bit more equal than the rest. No, I'm not taking away from defined leadership roles and decision-making power that a leader should have. But Saul's height symbolizes his supremacy over everyone else.

ONLY TWO WERE EQUIPPED

Saul was a gladiator. Other than his son, Jonathan, he was the only one carrying a sword. Nobody else could possess a weapon. Weapons of war were only for special people.

1 Samuel 13:22 describes it this way:

> *So it came about, on the day of battle, that there was neither sword nor spear found in the hand of any of the people who were with Saul and Jonathan. But they were found with Saul and Jonathan his son.*

What a way to fight a battle! How did Saul ever expect to win a war with this mentality?

Someone once said that if you want to have the tallest building in a city there are two ways to do it. You can either tear down every other building that's taller than yours, or you can simply build a bigger building than anyone else.

I think Saul's mindset was like the first one. He didn't want to have the tallest building, maybe, but he definitely wanted to remain the supreme leader. Instead of equipping everyone for battle by allowing weapons to be distributed among the nation, he simply would take away their weapons. This would make him the greatest warrior in the nation by default. Besides, giving others swords could be dangerous; someone might turn against him and try to take his throne by force.

Saul's kingship was driven by insecurity and fear. This insecurity drove him to push everyone around him down, while fear of the competition drove him to assign the exclusive right for fighting battles to himself and his son.

Unfortunately, the very sword that he exclusively kept to himself ultimately took his life.

LEADING BY INTIMIDATION

For a minute or two, Saul was actually anointed by God to be a king. Now, it certainly didn't last long, but for just a little while, he was actually an anointed man of God.

However, just because you are anointed, doesn't mean your character matches up with the anointing. Saul clearly wasn't that "man after God's own heart."

1 Samuel 11: 6 tells us the following story:

> *Then the Spirit of God came upon Saul when he heard this news, and his anger was greatly aroused. So he took a yoke of oxen and cut them in pieces, and sent them throughout all the territory of Israel by the hands of messengers, saying, "Whoever does not go out with Saul and Samuel to battle, so it shall be done to his oxen."*

Crazy, right? On the one hand, the Spirit of God came upon Saul, and on the other hand, Saul's anger was greatly aroused. So much so that he took a yoke of oxen and cut it in pieces. Then he gave those pieces to messengers who would rally the troops to go out to battle. Then he sent a warning that if someone would not listen, he would have their oxen cut up in pieces too.

In other words, he was leading through intimidation. He was a bully. If the people didn't follow his lead there would be consequences!

What a way to lead. It was his way or the highway.

Saul didn't want anyone trained for war, but when he needed help fighting a battle, he still demanded the people contribute to the fight. If not, it would hurt them!

Just because Saul was anointed king doesn't mean his character was developed. His fear and insecurity drove him to lead his people by intimidation.

Confusing: On the one hand, the Spirit of God was definitely evident. On the other hand, something was off.

Wrong behavior is never justified because someone is anointed. Saul was a clear example of that.

TAKING FOR HIMSELF

Saul ruled a kingdom that was self-serving. Everything in the kingdom ultimately was there to serve him. 1 Samuel 14:52 puts it this way:

> *Now there was fierce war with the Philistines all the days of Saul. And when Saul saw any strong man or any valiant man, he took him for himself.*

Anyone who had a gift or any value at all was claimed by Saul as his property. Anyone under him with any type of gifting was taken possession of.

Instead of releasing people into their own gifts and building their own lives with the talents that God had given them, he claimed it all for himself to help him build his little empire.

BOWING TO CULTURE, NOT GOD

Very early on in Saul's time as king, God already made a decision to reject him. 1 Samuel 13:7-14 tells us how this happened:

> *As for Saul, he was still in Gilgal, and all the people followed him trembling.*
>
> *Then he waited seven days, according to the time set by Samuel. But Samuel did not come to Gilgal; and the people*

*were scattered from him. So Saul said, "Bring a burnt
offering and peace offerings here to me." And he offered
the burnt offering.*

*Now it happened, as soon as he had finished presenting the
burnt offering, that Samuel came; and Saul went out to
meet him, that he might greet him.*

And Samuel said, "What have you done?"

*Saul said, "When I saw that the people were scattered from
me, and that you did not come within the days appointed,
and that the Philistines gathered together at Michmash,
then I said, 'The Philistines will now come down on me
at Gilgal, and I have not made supplication to the Lord.'
Therefore I felt compelled, and offered a burnt offering."*

*And Samuel said to Saul, "You have done foolishly. You
have not kept the commandment of the Lord your God,
which He commanded you. For now the Lord would have
established your kingdom over Israel forever. But now
your kingdom shall not continue. The Lord has sought for
Himself a man after His own heart, and the Lord has commanded him to be commander over His people, because you
have not kept what the Lord commanded you."*

Samuel had given Saul a clear instruction. He was to wait
for him before starting to sacrifice. However, when Saul's

obedience caused people to leave him, his insecurity pushed him to give the people what they wanted to prevent them from leaving.

Saul bowed to the demands of the people. He even explained his decision to Samuel; he said that it made sense in the moment. The people were leaving him, so he decided to give them what they wanted.

It was then that the prophet showed up and declared that Saul's kingdom was being rejected. When the demands of the nation became more important than the demands of God, the kingdom was taken from Saul.

THE PULL OF IRRATIONAL LOYALTY

Loyalty is great as long as it is rightly placed. Saul had a unique ability to create irrational loyalty from his son Jonathan.

As I observed earlier in this book, we are all sons of Saul; we are all like Jonathan. We find ourselves in the middle of a conflict.

It's interesting to read how Jonathan viewed and treated David. His loyalty to David was remarkable. 1 Samuel 20 describes some of the story in which Jonathan chose the well-being of David over the will of his father. And in 1 Samuel 23:16-18 he even takes it to the next level, straight out confessing what he believes about David's future:

> Then Jonathan, Saul's son, arose and went to David in the woods and strengthened his hand in God. And he said to him, "Do not fear, for the hand of Saul my father shall not find you. You shall be king over Israel, and I shall be next to you. Even my father Saul knows that." So the two of them made a covenant before the Lord. And David stayed in the woods, and Jonathan went to his own house.

It was clear to Jonathan that David would be the next king. He pledged allegiance to David by telling him that he would be right next to him. They even made a covenant that day.

Yet there was something about Saul that lured Jonathan back to his side. Despite the revelation that Jonathan had. Despite the loyalty to David that he had shown in the past. Despite the promises he made. And despite the covenant that was in place, when the rubber met the road, he made the irrational decision to join his father in battle, a choice which ended up costing his life.

There is something with "the house of Saul" that places a spell on people. Something that keeps them from separating themselves from it to pursue something that they know will be better. Saul demands irrational loyalty to the point of death and is somehow able to get it from his sons.

Like Jonathan, as we find ourselves in the middle of this conflict, we're going to have to deal with something that is incredibly strong, that wants to pull us right back into what we know has no future.

Don't end up like Jonathan who, despite knowing better, died as a result of his loyalty to the wrong thing.

THE JOURNEY TO TRUE KINGSHIP

In a way, I feel bad for Saul. He never had the ambition to become king; I'm sure it never even crossed his mind. 1 Samuel 9 and 10 tell the story of his journey to kingship, and it's rather a crazy one, to be honest.

There was Saul looking for his father's donkeys, which had been lost for unclear reasons. He had been looking for those donkeys for a while, but without any luck. Before they returned home, Saul's servant suggested that they visit Samuel as a final attempt and get some prophetic insight into the whereabouts of those animals.

The last thing on Saul's mind was what was about to happen next. Yes, the prophet provided prophetic insight on the whereabouts of the donkeys, but in addition to that, Samuel took a flask of oil and anointed Saul king of Israel. He also outlined what Saul was going to experience in the next seven days, which would confirm that what had just happened was real.

In 1 Samuel 10:9 we read:

> So it was, when he had turned his back to go from Samuel, that God gave him another heart; and all those signs came to pass that day.

Saul's journey to kingship was literally only seven days. In an instant, he was changed. He became an overnight sensation!

There was really nothing that could have prepared him for the task ahead. He didn't want it. In fact, he was insecure and hid himself among the supplies as Samuel was trying to find him to announce him as king in Mizpah.

He was set up to fail because he just wasn't prepared.

The truth is that there are no shortcuts to true kingship. There is a journey through which a king is developed. David didn't become a man after God's heart and mind in a moment. He had his flaws and character issues that he needed to deal with before he became that man.

Unlike Saul's journey, it took David decades to become king. David's journey slowly turned him into the man he needed to be in order to become a leader in God's kingdom.

The Bible teaches us that, when David was still very young, God started to prepare him for his future, at a time when he wasn't even aware of his destiny.

1 Samuel 17:34-36 recounts how David told Saul:

> *"Your servant used to keep his father's sheep, and when a lion or a bear came and took a lamb out of the flock, I went out after it and struck it, and delivered the lamb from its mouth; and when it arose against me, I caught it by its beard, and struck and killed it. Your servant has killed both lion and bear."*

David had won battles when nobody was watching that prepared him for battles he had to fight in the future. This qualified him for the next step in his journey—the call.

1 Samuel 16 tells how Samuel anointed David as king among a small circle of family. This wasn't a very public event. Only a few witnessed the moment when Samuel declared the destiny of the future king. No, David wasn't ready to be king yet, but the prophetic seed of his kingship was planted that day.

The anointing on his life became so evident that it opened doors for David. Big ones! He was invited to join Saul's worship team. David's music calmed Saul down when he became distressed, knowing the kingship had been taken from him.

Samuel the prophet had spoken; he knew it was just a matter of time before he would be removed from his throne. Yet the people hadn't caught up with the prophetic word that Saul knew would end his reign.

David served Saul with all his might, which I believe would ultimately qualify him to be that man after God's own heart.

When the opportunity arose, David volunteered to take on the giant Goliath. He was ready. He knew that in God's kingdom there was no place for fear. There was no room for God's people to be paralyzed by intimidation.

Goliath had been defying the ranks of God's army for too long. His words had pushed the army of Israel back over and over again. Every time the giant came out, God's people fled from him, dreadfully afraid. They spiraled down into an infinite loop of going out to the fight and shouting for the battle, just to run away in fear next.

This had been going on for forty days. The Israelites would gather their courage every morning during their prayer meeting. They would shout and declare things pertaining to their victory. Yet when their prayer meeting was over, they would retreat in fear. Nothing changed. The kingdom they represented was unable to break them free from their limitation. The words of Goliath kept them captive and paralyzed.

David was ready. He knew that Goliath was no match for the kingdom he represented.

Before he went out to face the giant, David was offered Saul's armor, considered the ultimate battle gear. It was seen as his only hope for survival. The likelihood of him beating Goliath was small, but wearing Saul's harness would at least give him a slim chance.

Yet, David shook off the traditional trappings of what was assumed would provide him victory. He knew he represented a different kingdom—one where his biggest asset was his individual, authentic self. And in due course a simple rock and a sling killed Goliath, delivering Israel from the grip of the Philistines.

THE PROMISE OF HEAVEN

Saul began to realize that this guy wasn't just another person on his worship team. There was something else going on here. He became intrigued with David and made him his armor bearer. Then he put him in charge of bigger projects and ultimately some major battles. David was able to deliver on every level, through every stage, as his responsibilities and public profile increased dramatically.

It came to the point where the people started to sense and see that this "David guy" was actually better than their own king.

Sure, Saul had defeated a thousand, but David . . . he defeated at least ten thousand!

So a song came forth. A song that effectively split the kingdom in two. Its echo has become the conflict we find ourselves in today. The war between the house of Saul and the house of David.

For David to stay in Saul's house would mean guaranteed death. He had to run, which pushed him into the next phase of his preparation to be king in Israel.

David had multiple opportunities to kill Saul and to take his throne before his time. Yet his strong character kept him from doing so. Instead, he started to congregate with others who had found themselves on the same side of the conflict, other misfits who were on the run from Saul as well.

They started "church" in a cave named Adullam. A place that slowly grew as new people were added daily—mighty men of valor who were captains in the army. They came to David to help him, until it was a great army, like the army of God.

The house of David became stronger and stronger as the house of Saul grew weaker and weaker, to the point where Judah started to recognize what God was doing through David. Judah decided to anoint David as king. But it wasn't until Saul fell on his own sword during his battle against the Philistines that the whole of Israel finally recognized David as the one true king.

He was prepared. Not just in seven days, but through a lifetime of preparation that made him the man—after God's own heart—for the job.

This kingdom that God promises us doesn't manifest overnight. It comes through a road of preparation that qualifies us and molds us into the men and women after God's heart that this kingdom requires. Perhaps you can look at these different phases that David went through and pinpoint where you are in the journey.

No, the pathway to kingship isn't always glamorous. Oftentimes it's hard. But be encouraged. At the end, it's all worth it. God's kingdom ultimately brings righteousness, peace, and joy to those who enter it.

Stay the course and hold fast to the promise of God. He wants to deliver to us a kingdom that will allow us to truly manifest as kings. Kings who can administrate His kingdom on earth, as it is already in heaven.

A JOURNEY INTO THE UNKNOWN

As you've been reading this book, you may have found yourself asking, *What does this all this mean practically?* I understand: we have the tendency to want to "fill in the blanks" and come up with "a formula" to define the "new normal."

But the truth is, we are going where no one has gone before. There is no point of reference for Jerusalem that will make our journey there easy.

In some ways, our journey is much like that for God's people the night they escaped Egypt. After carefully following every instruction from their fearless leader, Moses, they finally ended up leaving their place of limitation in the middle of the night. It was pitch black. They couldn't see anything ahead.

Isn't it interesting that the time of their deliverance was at the darkest hour of the day?

They couldn't see where they were going. It required faith and total surrender to what they believed God was directing them to do. Yet with every step they took, the sun came up a little more until they were walking in the bright of day.

Like the Israelites, we're leaving our status quo in the dark of night. We can't really see where we're going. We just know that we can't stay where we've been. At the risk of getting lost, we move forward into the unknown while the light starts to shine brighter and brighter with every step we take.

When we talk about Jerusalem and this kingdom we're believing for, we simply don't know what it will look like. Nobody has gone before us. We are those crying in the wilderness. Those who will turn undeveloped territory into the city of God.

Yet it will require faith. It will require everything to do so.

Regardless, God has made up His mind. He desires to deliver us a kingdom. One that is going to advance over the face of the earth. There is no stopping Him and His agenda. His Word cannot return void.

In Matthew 21:44, Jesus says in regards to the kingdom of God:

> *"And whoever falls on this stone will be broken; but on whomever it falls, it will grind him to powder."*

God's kingdom will advance. It will either break those who are willing to take the journey, or it will ultimately crush those who choose to hold on to the past.

The choice is yours. Either way it's going to hurt! Yet the payoff will be incredible.

This journey is not for the faint of heart. It's not going to be easy. It's going to cost a lot for whomever chooses to migrate to Jerusalem. Along the way, there will be questions. The fear of the unknown will try to paralyze you.

We will feel scared. We will feel insecure. Even David felt insecure in his journey to kingship. On the surface it all seemed like he was the poster child of "the confident leader," yet even he was plagued by doubts and uncertainties.

Yes, he was anointed by Samuel. Yes, he defeated the lion, the bear, and even Goliath. Even Saul's son, Jonathan, saw the writing on the wall, that David was destined to be king over Israel. Yet even when Judah and ultimately Israel acknowledged and anointed David as king, it still wasn't enough to deal with his insecurity.

It wasn't until Hiram, king of Tyre sent messengers that David's insecurity was finally dealt with.

In 1 Chronicles 14:1-2 we read:

> "*Now Hiram king of Tyre sent messengers to David, and cedar trees, with masons and carpenters, to build him a house.* So David knew that the Lord had established him as king over Israel, *for his kingdom was highly exalted for the sake of His people Israel* (emphasis added).

It wasn't until another king sent messengers, as well as a bunch of supplies and experts, to build David a house that he finally "knew" that he was king. Despite his victories, he continued to struggle with accepting his identity as king.

There is uncertainty and ambiguity ahead of us. No one man has the answer to all questions. The day of the solo gladiator is over. Shiloh will no longer be the seat of government. Jerusalem will facilitate an environment where the body of Christ can congregate and collectively put definition to what the future will look like.

On the path to Jerusalem, we will connect to those who have decided to take the same journey. One will bring one piece of the puzzle while another brings another. Malachi 3:16 offers a picture of what that can look like:

> *Then those who feared the Lord spoke to one another, And the Lord listened and heard them; So a book of remembrance was written before Him For those who fear the Lord And who meditate on His name.*

The Lord will listen as we try to figure out the future. He will provide revelation along the way so we can start documenting the "new normal" and write a book that will serve as a point of reference for the future. There will be questions, but collectively we will find the answers. Let's just not be too quick to fill in the blanks. Let's "speak to one another" before we determine what the future should look like.

No, it's not all clear right now. But one thing I know for sure. It will be bright. It will be better.

Let's move into the future together. Let's shift!

YOU HAVE A MESSAGE THAT NEEDS TO BE HEARD

It's time to innovate the way we package our message and bring it to market!

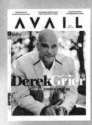

AVAIL +

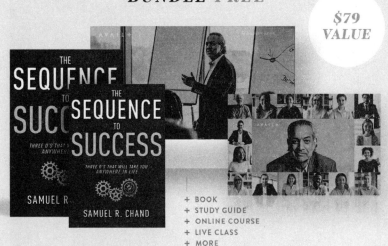